The Black Book of the Programmer_

The Black Book of the Programmer
How to have a successful career developing software
and how to avoid common mistakes

Rafael Gómez Blanes

© Rafael Gómez Blanes, 2018

contact@rafablanes.com

www.rafablanes.com

To my girls: Luna and Beatriz

Table of contents

HAVE YOU EVER FELT LIKE THIS?

The Black Book of the Programmer will show you what
distinguishes a good software professional from the one that
just "plays" with technology without finding the important
results: that we work with high productivity in the new
working paradigm for what is indispensable: cultivating
good and productive work habits.

*The author_*

I am a Superior Computer Engineer from Seville's University. Nowadays I work on software development and Solid Stack's business developer (a company that has just been formalized and belong to Telecontrol STM).

I worked for twelve years for an engineering company (Telvent Energy) and I have participated on more projects than I can remember. I've been interested for many years on everything related to clean code, agile practices, and good work procedures and, specially, creating values through software.

I have also participated on many international projects and live in Sweden for a year and a half.

I was born in Seville (Spain) and I live on a little town at the province's north with my family, my garden and more wild animals than I'd like.

www.solid-stack.com

*Introduction_*

It's been three years since I first published The Black Book of the Programmer and I can happily say that it has been kind of successful, because of the scarce literature in Spanish about the conditions that surround a good software project.

Three years in software is enough to separate prehistory from a future that I, after almost twenty years working as a software engineer, still find fascinating, especially because it's full of opportunities for everything technology related. Nevertheless, I still perceive very little interest in truly exploiting the opportunities in an activity that is actually more transversal than ever, because definitely, everything, to a greater or lesser extent, is dominated by projects that are made of thousands and thousands of code lines.

I have seen, since the first edition, that some emerging technologies suddenly were from one day to the other very popular and vice versa; I have also had the opportunity to prove why software projects deteriorate because of a poorly driven organic growth.

But above all, I have proved firsthand again that work, design and methodologic principles have just vary and they are still the cornerstone of success in our profession, but still they are almost unknown between the people who have been on our activity for some time and the ones that have just finished their academic stage.

That is precisely what this book is about, everything that surrounds the construction of good software.

In The Black Book of the Programmer you will not find a single code line but you'll learn what it means to program and how to do it right.

Also, you are not going to find a debate for or against some technologies, but it will help you to choose them wisely. You'll realize that you don't need to be some kind of guru to have a massive success on everything you set your mind into as a programmer.

Even so, we can't go against the industry, against a sector that moves toward the creation of bigger and more scalable systems and where the dispersion of technologies is even bigger than three years ago. In this time, the cloud world has matured even more with a lot of new services and more competitive prices, advancing at an unstoppable pace. Anyway, software, infrastructure and platform like services (Saas, Iaas, Paas) are now a more tangible reality, and everything related to microservices based design, as well as a DevOps culture, has been dusted off from the library of history to return to the present with concepts developed some time ago. And that's how we turn the mantra word that, without a doubt, will be known by everyone soon: blockchain, on the new paradigm that promises to change the internet confidence schemes.

On this time, in which I have also published a novel

(www.gblanes.com), and harvested many useful comment about bookselling, I have assumed failure in some initiatives, but also a great success in others that, at this moment, keep me alive and willing to demonstrate that you can make quality software without it, necessarily, implying a costs' increase, which is what I do in the company where I participate: Solid Stack (www.solid-stack.com).

Thank you for your interest in this book.

If you want to substantially improve your career as a software developer, keep reading!

Rafa G. Blanes

www.rafablanes.com

*Warming up to start_*

«Use your time to cultivate yourself through the
writings
of others, so you will easily earn what has been a
tough task for us.»

(Sócrates)

We are living exciting moments: a new economic paradigm has come to stay, we can hire almost any service from anywhere in the world, we can also design and make custom made commissions from thousands of miles away and what you fabricate and produce in your company can be commercialized in many parts of the world. Professions that did not exist before are now common (data scientist, community manager, etc.), a high work rotation is making "lifetime" job positions obsolete, there's who defines all this scenario as a crisis, others as a paradigm and a new order full of opportunities. There are many options to choose.

However, all of this has been possible thanks to the global display of communication networks that shows us opportunities that were unimaginable before. Some say that everything we are living right now is a natural consequence of the implantation and use of the Internet. And everything goes faster since the cloud increases its services and benefits just as they lower their prices.

The protagonist of this silent revolution is, essentially, software development: everything around us is computerized but still the computer profession suffers of some kind of misunderstanding from the rest of society: software developers are easily pigeonholed, they are associated with a frivolous image of "youth", of working in old garages when actually a good project only gets ahead with a high degree of specialization and experience.

Are we aware of the enormous facility that we have nowadays to launch and get innovative ideas started from the hall of our homes? that the entry barriers of many businesses have fallen precipitously? Are we aware that all this revolution is being starred by the software that is being executed in millions of servers around the world?

According to a study published recently, in the USA the workforce that works "developing applications" is now greater than the number of workers dedicated to agriculture, isn't it surprising? Likewise, I can't stop reading that software development will be one of the most demanded careers in a close future, which is now happening, but in form of web analysts, SEO (search engine optimization), big data experts, etc. It is a profession for the future indeed but I wonder which will be the characteristics that will distinguish a good professional from others whose work is not enough.

However, reality is sometimes very frustrating: the power of technology would vanish if it didn't have the support of thousands of software developers striving day by day so it would not collapse, making hotfixes or shabby solutions, maintaining in extremis the applications whose organic growth have turned into an unmanageable spaghetti, evolving those dreadful websites whose companies want to make rentable or developing apps to obtain some passive income... it is a polyhedral profession, multidisciplinary, in which you can dedicate yourself to do loads of extraordinarily different stuff. But all, absolutely all, has to be well done, with professionality, if we are capable of surrounding ourselves with good habits and understanding the fragile, artistic and creative nature of software.

And then comes the chain of command... when the good technical work and the years of experience developing efficient and right software architecture is thrown away it's because the only way of prospering (understood as earning more money, logically), is passing to "the next level" as a manager and starting to work with something an computer developer barely knows, something that is scarcely taught academically: managing a working team.

But, what does developing SOA architecture, implementing a minimum viable product or extreme methodology has to do with managing the time and work of a team of people, which, in its majority, look at you with apprehension because, for them, earning more money means doing what you had just achieved? And even worst, when this happens in a professional context (like the one of the 2008's crisis) where the general environment is everyone clinging to their positions and defending them with nails and teeth if they have to, while salaries for a software developer or engineer, do not precisely stand out, at least in the Hispanic world.

In these lamentable cases, the dominant business mentality that rewards you when you assume more "responsibility" makes you lose a wonderful technician or win a dreadful manager. I have seen it before with all its disastrous results. This has happened to me and is a usual situation in the sector. However, what a disgrace these dynamic and inertia is to programming! Because, if they pay you more for "managing and coordinating" it would be that other stuff is less important... It is hard to find someone with a better economic retribution programming than managing work groups or projects.

So, what professional future can be expected from a passionate technology lover that spends many hours in front of a computer screen debbugabling a subtle mistake or from someone that strives to generate the most maintainable and light software but neither his boss nor his client will appreciate it because all they care about is measuring time and costs in short term (which is, otherwise, logic)?

The software development is a profession for the present and with an enormous future, notwithstanding, we do not know how to make the most of this new economic paradigm full of opportunities: we always make the same mistakes, over and over again, without realizing that the only competitive advantages that we'll have will be quality and innovation and, of course, entrepreneurship, because now more than ever it is easier to test a business idea and get it started with few resources.

That is why I present this book, where I resume my, more or less, dilated work experience, as a freelancer, project manager, software architect and also, responsible of business development, a path with many disappointing failures, mistakes and deceptions, but also full of professional successes that allow me to keep on loving my daily activity.

In The Black Book of the Programmer you will find the most common mistakes that we make as professional software developers and, essentially, how to avoid them. The most interesting part is that the majority of these mistakes, stumbles and problems that end up making a project fail are not of technical character.

Different from other professions, the vocational factor in software development is important: the best developers are the ones that truly enjoy what they do. And, shouldn't we all want to love everything we do? Or do we have to conform working eight or more hours a day selling our time to pay the bills? We are going toward a kind of economy where the time we spent working will be more and more irrelevant: the important thing will be the results and the objectives met; we will be paid for "projects" and the payroll employment will be increasingly scarce just for the structural staff required to maintain the survival of the company (see the book "Free Agent Nation" (1) by Daniel H. Pink).

Here it goes the exciting journey of a computer engineer obsessed with showing the special idiosyncrasy of our profession and, above all, teaching that there are many non-technical circumstances that "surround" our activity and determine our success or failure.

I want to also show in which terms a software solution should be considered correctly realized as an "artistic" part of the process more than a technical one. For the ones that still don't realize we, the software developers, are more like artists than cold mathematical minds. We create artifacts out of nowhere that have to evolve and maintain for a long time.

Simplicity, emerging designs, technical doubt, the good developer habits, team work, refactoring, testable software development, methodologic profitability, hours or productivity, good organization, abstraction under principles, work discipline, reutilization and decoupling of modules and libraries, (and a long etcetera) are the ingredients and the regular vocabulary with which I hope to create, shape and motivate more and better professionals.

This book is written by a software developer for other programmers and developers. I firmly believe that the best curriculum that we can show is a good work realized with the maximum quality and, especially, of enormous utility. It depends of us, to some extent, to surround ourselves with the adequate "conditions" to reach this objective.

The Black Book of the Programmer's Manifesto_

You have in your hands a book that will improve radically how you act as a software developer: the following chapters will show you the "ground" you have to harvest in order to make maximum quality projects and substantially improve your career as a professional programmer.

The difference between being a low class programmer, maybe frustrated with his profession and being a software developer with many successes behind is a matter of simple work habits y, above all, knowing that software has its own, not only technical but creative and artistic idiosyncrasy. Hence the following manifesto of The Black Book of the Programmer, a whole declaration of principles.

Professional software development has as many creative and artistic aspects as technical.

We receive a many years formation in order to obtain a great deal of knowledge that we will hardly applicate later on.

We develop projects in companies that do not know about the evanescent and fragile nature of a well-developed software product applying industrial production criteria.

We like to investigative (which is good) and bragging (which is not) about the knowledge of all the emerging technology. We are, in some ways, victims of a kind of childish dilettantism.

We show spectacular results when internally the fragility level of an application will make you throw it away after some months because of its unsustainability.

We often forget that any success in software (and other professions as well) is a mix of technology, talent and methodology. Nothing slightly complex can be realized without a previous script or framework that allows us to make things organized (methodology).

Generally, bosses and decision layers don't have a clear view of the creative and artistic nature off software development.

In our academic stage we are not taught to do teamwork or that the success of a software project depends on the collaboration between all its members.

Some like to be seen as gurus, full of pride when people recognizes them as it, but whose individualism does not allows them to work successfully inside a team.

We confuse meeting the dates with delivering a quality product.

Sometimes we like to be indispensables and do things convolutely to appropriate ourselves with a power parcel (turning into our own slaves).

We do not take enough advantage of the enormous entrepreneur capacity that we can have applying our technology knowledge in an economy that moves towards the digital domain: in the future, "talent" will distinguish professionals from non-professionals.

Therefore, we need a book that collects all of these reflections and teaches us how to approach all of these aspects of a profession that isn't socially valued nor economically rewarded enough.

Have you felt identified with any of the postulates of the – manifesto? We will see throughout the chapters of The Black Book of the Programmer how to correct the bad vices of our profession, for example, like that business culture that sometimes treats software without considering its nature for its adequate development and managing and, above all, we'll see which are the true habits that a good programmer has to harvest to do his job extraordinarily well and prosper.

I firmly believe that software development has more art characteristics than technical science ones, we construct more than we calculate and create more than we assemble.

Development, tests, refactoring (all in the same package) _

There's occasions when a software project ends up turning into an abandoned garden full of weeds. I have a house with a kind of large gardened area; it's amazing to see how nature proliferates by itself, at its own rate, if you let it grow to its taste. In a few weeks, some big weeds with pointy leaves will start to invade the grass slowly, some cute little plants which species I still can't identify appear here and there, soon these harmless weeds will reach a considerable seize. Scattered pieces of grass grow at its whim and create big manes that, if you don't act on time, will make you use a big hoe to eliminate them, leaving a hole in the ground. If you do not do anything in months, what was a piece of plain piece of ground will take an irregular vegetable orography , if time keeps on passing, in less than we imagined, where my daughters could play before will turn into a completely impassable zone.

That's when the situation cannot wait any longer and, with more obligation than desire, you decide to spend Saturday and Sunday cleaning the vegetable disaster before the neighbors mistake your house with the one from "Jumanji" (movie that I love, by the way). With great effort and tedium, you got to dedicate yourself thoroughly to clean the weeds clearing everywhere. The work is exhausting and it only serves you to go back to the starting situation from months ago; if you do not decide to use some potent herbicides, you will return to the same position after a while.

Well, that is how software development evolves very often. If a had dedicated to the pleasant hobby of domestic gardening long before, the situation would have not deteriorated that much, it wouldn't have reached that frustrating weekend and the piece of ground would've relatively conserved itself clean from the weeds with a lot less effort.

And many times we don't know how to value the "hidden cost" that not doing something has. What in small doses was approachable and even enjoyable (relaxing gardening exercises) can turn into an authentic nightmare later on.

The question here is if we have incorporated or not some habits to prevent these situations and reduce productivity to its maximum expression.

As software developers, we experience exactly the same: we do not know (or we have not been taught) well enough what our good day-by-day habits should be like to prevent an application from turning into a dump impossible to fix over time.

When we start a new solution, we like to start to key lines and lines of code for anxiety of having (and even showing) something working as soon as possible, or for the contrary we suddenly find ourselves with all the work accumulated as the expected delivery dates are approaching.

We go on generating "production" software without making sure enough that what we are building has to be tested with the correct warranty. How many of us have not done the typical console program out of solution to probe something specific?

This is one of our major vices: we create production software without software that proves it or supports it and shows us to ourselves that it works. I have spent a lot of time analyzing why this happens this way, why is it so hard for the team that you work with to not abandoning the test development at any phase of the project and what is not little, that the quality of these tests is the adequate.

Theory shows us that a good development team has its own testers who are responsible for writing the tests to support the work of the rest of the developers; however, reality is quite different: in very few projects I've seen a specific tester role and a lot less someone with a SQA profile (software quality and assurance)

The main reason to obviate test development as we make

production software is that we are used to make "not test-focused" software: indeed, to generate tests that can be automatically reproduced over and over again it's required that the software that you develop is testable. For that, the way to abstract a problem and turn it into code pieces has to change necessarily. An application can work efficiently but it cannot be written in a way that automatic test could be made to test its behavior.

The design and nature of testable software is completely different from a code made without the continuous habit of test support. Read this again because the basic key for a quality project is at this point.

The second reason (but not less important) is that we do not perceive the "hidden cost" that not implementing tests has: we let the weeds grow week after week until the moment that we start to raise exotic animals in the jungle in which your garden has become or we have to hire someone to do a deep cleaning (at an infinitively major cost than doing a little cleaning job once in a while ourselves). This, translated to a software project is the same than throw it away sooner or later.

The third reason (and trust me, is the one I like the less) is that nobody obligates us: if you do not coexist with a working team centered in doing production software supported by tests, you are not likely to become into the eccentric that advances toward that direction, unless your boss or manager explicitly obligates you to do it; and even in that case, how does your manager control the tests quality or coverture that you do without dedicating 100% to it?

Here I presented three reasons that can be resumed into just one, a lot simpler: we do not implement tests because we don't have the habit of develop them.

If we did, it would be exactly the same as not brushing our teeth after lunch: you remain with an uncomfortable and strange item until you brush them, at least it happens to me, and I cannot sleep if I haven't brushed my teeth before.

Similarly, I couldn't possibly feel comfortable if I do not back up the code I write sufficiently with its corresponding tests. Any project or prototype that I do, almost since the first module or class, has its back up on tests that guarantee me to keep on adding functionality without breaking the previous one. I am no hero because of that, at all, I have simply learned with the years that the cost of not doing it that way is much bigger.

Mistakes intensify when we start to have less time for all the work ahead: stress and hasting hinder progress on development tasks or impede the maturing of design decisions, proving the best solution and, why not, the creation of good unitary tests, of integration, of validation, of regression, etc.

Advancing in the development with quality tests is something we have to incorporate to our DNA as developers; nowadays there's no excuse for using third tools or strange tests frameworks because those are not sufficiently known and mature when they are not integrated on the same development IDE.

Here, the habit is key and the deep knowing that if you do not support your software with tests, the time cost, hours, quality, euros and unsatisfied clients will be much bigger and could end up ruining the project. I have seen how some works have succeeded (they have given themselves in time and the client has been satisfied), but have failed later because there is no way to evolve them with new characteristics. What is the result? A new project thrown away and many time and euros wasted in the way.

Sometime I read a statistic about car brands for which the reparation invoices were lower: it coincided with the car brands and models that were easier to repair. This looks so evident, why we do not perceive it as professional programmers? Our software will be better (inexpensive) if it is easy to repair (debuggle).

Alright, now we know that the architecture and design of a susceptible application if it is proved by means of tests has nothing to do with the ones from an application which rigid design does not permit to generate tests. In this last case, the only possible tests are manual, but we don't want to do repetitive work but concentrate our efforts in the creativity of problem solving, or do we?

What often escapes us is that testable software has to have a structure, design and conception that are testable!; this is exactly the same that differences car models that are easier to repair from those that are an authentic martyrdom to even substitute a beam.

We can only create probable software if we abstract the solution well enough to then permit the development of the correspondent proves and that requires of a completely different mentality at the time of proposing and resolving problems.

Mentality and major abstraction, yes, but also knowing of important elements in the enginery of software, such as principles, design patterns, etc., of which I speak more carefully in the chapter "Everything is a matter of principles".

This needs practice but above all of wanting and having the firm purpose of "re-learn" our craft to permit the advancing of our productive code with tests.

Some years ago, I started an important reform of our house that my couple and I had been planning for quite a long time. We changed the kitchen to another place, looked for the best distribution for all the stuff and analyzed every detail so the enormous money inversion (and effort) that the reform supposed to us gave us exactly the kind of home that we were looking for. Well, despite having planned it all in extreme detail, after a year we realized that we putted a mosquito net on an interior window that did not really need it (...), taking out the tableware from the dishwasher machine turns into a marathon because the fitment where the tableware and glasses are stored is at the other extreme of the kitchen, one of the windows faces a large foliage tree that impedes the entry of enough natural light.

Once that you realize that these mistakes were not predicted, you can't go back without it supposing another headache or economic pain: hence you stay where you are and always find consolation saying "what a shame that we didn't realize that..."

Nevertheless, in software we have the ability and capacity to destruct, reconstruct and modify what we develop as we like: in fact, this improvement modification is not a step backward, but a jump forward if it supposes a design improvement or a solution implementation. It is an inversion even though sometimes it takes us a lot to eliminate or modify something that costs us hours or days to develop.

We call this technique "refactoring" and it consists just in looking for improvement or simplification of what we already have developed.

It is all a classic the book by Martin Fowler titled "Refactoring: improving the design of existing code"; this book has helped me like no other to improve the quality of the code that I write and should be in the bookshelves of any professional programmer.

The result of refactoring our solution with common sense is that this will have a cleaner design, be more testable and comprehensible, it will have less duplicities and will generally solve problems more easily, facilitating its evolution to the future to another member of the team, among many other arguments in favor of refactoring or not. I consider this theme crucially important, so much that I dare to say "I program, ergo I factor"; one thing goes along with the other. The development of tests will indicate us which parts of the system should be improved. And it is that this happens to be another one of the development pillars of mature and professional software: we refactorize as we advance generating a better solution each time.

We create production software, we prove it with tests that we can automatize and we stop for a second and ask ourselves "can I improve this or that?" These are the habits that we should incorporate to our programming art; the debt of not including them to our professional programmer's DNA is too high.

When I comment about these concepts people often surprise me saying that incorporating those habits "delays us" to generate the solution, but I absolutely disagree with that. The technical doubt of not programming test-orientated soon will make us have a solution infinitely more difficult to maintain, evolve and prove, going back to the 20/80 Pareto's relationship, which in its particular version for software means that we spend 20% of our time writing productive code and the other 80% debuggabling it! (Correcting mistakes), when what we want to achieve is precisely to invert this tendency. How? I believe that I have made this sufficiently clear: supporting our software with automatized tests as we advance and before taking a new step, refactoring and simplifying as continuous habits. The solution will generate a better design every time and winning in quality while the code will gain in cleansing and naivety.

Key points_

✓ It is indispensable to advance in the new code we incorporate to our project supporting it with tests; these could be of the same quality of the production code.

✓ The cost of not supporting in greater or lesser extent our project with tests could suppose its life-time to be shorter: it will be more expensive and harder to evolve and maintain and it surely will arrive to the client with non-detected mistakes.

✓ Before taking something for finished like, for example, a new class or functionality, we have to ask ourselves if there's anything we can do to improve it or simplify it. It's surprising to realize that refactoring, in the majority of occasions, supposes actually little work.

✓ If in our working team there's not yet any stablished solid culture of tests creation, we should try to stablish it: the quality of what we generate will be better and ultimately, we will pass less time detecting and correcting mistakes when the project passes to production.

✓ They have to be quality tests: they should also be

refactored as the project advances.

✓ We have to ask continuously to ourselves questions like "can I simplify this code in any way?" or "can this be easily understood by other people?"

✓ It is indispensable to program right, know all the necessary techniques to refactorize and generate a clean code.

*What is having success on a softwart project_*

Software can be delivered on time and still be a complete and absolute failure, simple as that, and at the same time, paradoxical as that.

Many times I have asked myself what determines the success of a project. Surprisingly it is not delivering it on time on the agreed terms,   there's infinity of subtle underlying factors that really indicate the level of failure or success reached.

I had the luck (or bad luck) some years ago of working on an international project that "initially" and seen from the outside, could see very thrilling. I counted with an experienced team, the latest technologies, a whole year ahead of time and all the necessary resources. There was finally a group of testers! I think I remember that we were more than twelve people involved.

Nevertheless, after ten months it became evident that

what had started with great expectative was going to end up on a big failure, a huge and monumental failure; then the problem would not be if we would finish on time or not, because it was clear that we were not but whose heads would roll... Then we centered on an "every man for him!" dynamic. An all rule failure and, nonetheless, that project taught me so many things that I really am grateful for that experience that stressed me that much: after making that many mistakes (and also after seeing how others put a grain of sand on that subject) I learned many of the abilities and positive habits that I apply since then.

"Resilience" is the name of the capacity of learning from one's mistakes and recovering from failure and since we work on a discipline in which the mistakes mechanisms are at hand and are very ethereal, a good software developer should have this capacity obligatorily: learning more from one's mistakes than from one's success. This is a reason why, the proudest people that I have met on this business are, in my opinion, the worst professionals.

I am convinced that software development is one of the professions in which more fails are accumulated; therefore, a good engineer has to develop a great resilience capacity (that is, enduring the downpour when required).

Parting from a promising project, with resources and enough time ahead, everything ended up with a totally "burned" team (the burnout syndrome was quite evident), doing extra time that, of course, wasn't going to be paid, on a very hostile Martian environment and where nobody no longer spoke but barked, meetings ended up on a corollary of personal accusations and the aversion between key members of the team was getting bigger day by day. It looks exaggerate that I put it this way, but I assure you that the tension on the air was tangible. Logically this situation affected negatively the development of the project.

I was one of those "key members" of the team (even though I am not that sure of it now!) so I suffered this situation maybe even more than the rest when I noticed that it was impossible to reach the project's common objectives this way, because it was not more than that: a common objective for the group of people that worked on it; therefore, the team's tuning will terminate on better results.

Failure was more than evident but it was not that easy to elucidate with the code's "quality" loss that was being develop under the influence of an extremely hostile environment like that. The decision layers, at the moment obsessed with delivering the results on time, were light years apart from understanding that. Anyhow, would it had been considered a success if it had been delivered on time? If it had been so, the manager, the director and some other more above would had been satisfied, having no clue of the poisoned heritage of the delivered.

A software project cannot be considered successful even if it is delivered on time when the team that develops it works with burnout syndrome all the time, the hostility and hermeticism between the developers are huge and when many of them just wait for the littlest blunder of a partner to hide up their own miseries. Subtly, on an environment like that, what will be develop will be a dreadful quality code, fragile and with tendency to the design corruption. Necessarily, the develop solution ill lack of the fundamental pillars of good software.

Thereby the way to the code's "spaghettitation" is served and assured (allow me this culinary reference, the "spaghetti" software is a concept that we should all know). There was no code homogenization, it could be noticed from anywhere anyone had put a step in among other niceties.

There's nothing new with this since similar situations occur in many working contexts, but on software this destructive dynamic has no tangible consequences from the beginning and not that easy to detect short term, even when they become exponentially evident long term.

The "art of programming" requires of a highly creative, lucid, calm, optimistic and positive environment. Actually, when we develop a solution, an API, a module a class, an algorithm or any device known by us, we are projecting the state of mind of that moment while we write lines and lines of code; we design something classy when our mind works and flows with enough calmness and relaxation.

Saving the distances, if a programmer does not completely suffer from the blank page syndrome that the writers fear that much, our particular blank page consists on a poor design, inconsistencies, mistakes that will face us sooner or later, code rigidness, excessive decoupling between modules, etc.

We cannot compare something done with "love" to something that we fabricated waiting for the clock to mark the end of the workday, rushing and without a single connection with what we do. I am not saying that we should think about this precious code lines on Valentine's Day... but we have to understand that we can only shine and do something excellently if we like it, if we are passionate about it.

Also, we cannot expect to have enough inspiration to reach that classy and simple solution that we need if our mind is invaded by problems and conflicts on the work group while we nudge the person next to us (figuratively, of course). A lot less we are going to have the spur and motivation necessary to refactor, for example, deleting this evident duplicity, anyway, why if I just want it to be 5 o'clock to leave? (I hope that the irony is understood).

Therefore, even if the project had been delivered on time and if the managers had hung their selves some medals for "tighten the team" the delivered product would have been of a dreadful quality; the mid- term consequences of this for a software project are nefarious. It is delivered on time, yes, but what is being given is a poisoned apple.

It is well known that, facing excessive pressure, we tend to relax on tests development (if they are ever made), we start to forget the numerous "to do's", comments that we constantly leave among the code lines as we get closer to the "happy path" when something has to be tested. This last point is a usual tendency when pressure watches us: proving the "happy path", when we are relaxing on the tests and the few we do are precisely the ones that we unconsciously know that will give us less problems.

This dynamic or inertia is suffered by any software team role: developer, tester, etc.

The result is an extremely fragile solution, made on the rush and to get out of the way; instead of a skyscraper (which is what we pretend to do at the beginning of a project), we end up delivering a shabby little adobe house that will disintegrate to the foundations when it rains.

In many cases and under these circumstances where we have delivered something worthy on time, this is evident, because even the most ingenuous manager would have made sure that the thing works before considering it finished or advancing to the next stage; so, where is the poisoned heritage? It probably was delivered an extremely fragile solution given under pressure, on the rush and by a jaded team of burnt people, a solution that will break down when the smallest changes are demanded from it, when the client's validation test battery slightly changes or when what is done has to evolve toward new unpredicted characteristics. On a hostile work environment, whatever the nature of it is, none of the agile software and "extreme" programming characteristics can be implemented: good practices and habits that increase quality and productivity at many levels.

That's when the forming satisfied face of the managers, directors, bosses, and... (Why is there always a command chain and why is it that long?), that satisfaction faces, I mean, will turn into worrying faces, of general embarrassment, when they observe that the adaptation, improvement or correction times are getting extremely and abnormally long. It has been delivered, definitely, a neither evolvable nor maintainable solution. Bread from today and hunger from tomorrow... on this way the initial delivery was surely a success (it was delivered on time) but then we realize the underlying rottenness.

Effectively, the psychological conditioners that surround the act of programming matter. A developer cannot implement a clean code with a whip behind. Some time I read that some enterprise measured their employees' productivity (sadly) with the number of lines they wrote.

A programming professional does not execute a beautiful and elegant solution when he knows that it will not be valued by the team, of which he can suspect that they want to appropriate it. Nothing can be created, no software, no art, not even a garden looking for the excellence on a demotivating and non-creative environment. On software, "beautiful and elegant" means easy and inexpensive to evolve and maintain. I don't get tired of insisting on it.

This situation repeats itself on many occasions and it will

continue to happen because the "maintainable" and essentially simple nature that any delivered software solution should have isn't completely understood. It is like buying and unrepairable car! It is not understood neither that it is hard to value and verify the quality of a developer's work, even when well-known metrics are used. To evaluate this quality takes a lot of software experience and, sadly, the business dynamic in which we move makes the managers, coordinators and bosses lack of this experience and be more centered on managing tasks, endless meetings and meet the dates "either way".

When the poisoned heritage explodes, the original team has already been discomposed into pieces (some even may have changed companies) and the problem, that has probably turned into a huge problem by then, will fall into another team that has nothing to do with the subject, starting again with short and insufficient times, and destined to repeat the same story, eternally hitting the same stone; meanwhile, the costs keep getting higher (at the same rate as pressure increases over the team of developers).

Behind this dynamic there's people that even wanting to do their job right are not offered the conditions for develop it with quality and pulchritude. Does the company provide the adequate conditions to develop quality software?

However, there's people who has to be responsible of offering and fomenting this working environment, but generally this people is busy with other stuff (like pushing harder with some unpredictable thing, for example). It is a problem of business culture and organization coaching. Even though the developer should also please a nice working environment with his attitude, a good manager should detect friction situations and create a cooperative environment and promote the welfare of his team: it is part of his role.

The professional that perceives this and has experience enough to guess the final title of the movie, incapable of changing these conditions and dynamics, is definitively and underutilized professional, a wasted and frustrated resource: it is an employee that suffers and goes home stressed out. This is the profile of the software engineer that suffers from the sensation of being paid for doing the humdrum job of "cutting code" instead of being paid for his true job of design and enginery.

The project may be delivered in time, but I tis a failure by itself because of the trail of personal suffering, lack of quality, vulnerability and fragility of the delivered product, all of that will make the maintenance costs and mid to long term evolution very much major.

In the current economy we can only choose to compete with quality or quantity. I prefer the first (trusting that the serious enterprises too), although at the same time I know that quantity depends on a matter of productivity.

Here is a professional wisdom gem: if you detect that you are on a similar situation, then you know the ending; your responsibility is to alert the responsible, convince the rest of the team to work that way and, why not, a professional does not waste his time on projects that are dirty with mud. If the team's profile is not compatible, the manager should restructure it, as simple as that.

About the international project that I was talking about at the beginning: I asked for a location change on the enterprise.

☐

Key points_

✓ Software development is a highly creative activity; so it needs an environment that does not destroy or asphyxiate creativity but foments it.

✓ If we have to rush to "deliver" at all costs according to the planned dates, it is evident that someone planned the work and dates incorrectly.

✓ Working fast and with stress chronically on the project will cause the quality of the generated software to be infinitely minor than working at a right and more relaxed rate.This lack of quality translates on money: major future cost for correcting mistakes, major number of mistakes, major problems to evolve the system, unsatisfied clients because of the lack of quality, etc.

✓ As professionals we should foment a right and

adequate environment with the working team; when it is impossible we have to understand that it hurts us as professionals and, therefore, it must be considered to leave the project or even the company.

✓ Curriculum is only validated by quality, not the quantity of projects poorly finished and problematic.

*Everything is a matter of principles_*

One time I found an application whose authors counted with a very good company consideration. The software worked, that was evident, because it was being exploited on many diverse installations, but he time a partner and I spent trying to decipher its functioning for its evolution clearly didn't; they asked us to add a new functionality an even being a non-complex system, we struggled a lot to understand the general structure and how and where to apply the changes.

The project was on Java, and used Java Beans with an Oracle data base. This application connected to the national electric operator and participated on the energy trading at the electric market. What I want to imply here is that its functioning had an important economic impact.

When you read good literature you can appreciate and intuit much more information than the author that literally plasm on the text; a tale, without going further, is so much more than the story of some charismatic characters with a happy ending: there's a moral and a lection that is extracted from it but it is implicit and we have to discover it, it is suggested more than it is explicitly indicated. That's how good literature works, good narrative says a lot more than what is explicitly read. Also, it does it with an all, it's not enough to read a paragraph to have a clear idea of the story's quality but it is the harmony and the structure of the whole what gives it solidity.

On software happens exactly the same, and for this reason I consider that the developers are somehow like "authors": when we read a code realized by others we can get into the tangled and confusing minds of the programmers or enter a paradise of calm and simplicity where someone worried enough to leave things clean and easy to digest. A good code, as well as the moral of the story, reveals implicitly the "design intention".

This is on of the big differences between good and bad software. Or what is the same, an application that realizes complex operations does not have to have been implemented on a complicated and hermetic way; on the contrary, even the hardest could and should be resolved on a simple way.

It is true that the functioning could be equally right to an application resolved on a abstruse way and to other that does exactly the same but whose design is simpler, classier and easy. Systems can work anyway, no doubt, but the effort, dedication and surely frustration to understand the developed can be very different.

I still do not understand why many developers that sin a little of arrogance and presume about how good they are, end up writing a hard to understand code to everyone..., except for themselves.

I do not know if there is any relation or not, I would like that it does not, however, solving a complex problem on an easy way has more geniality than solving it with something intrinsically hard to comprehend. The genius of a good software developer is in knowing how to find simple solutions no matter how complicated the problem could be. If it is complex, it should be divided on simpler sub problems. This is an unquestionable principle for me and I repeat it to myself like a mantra while I am at work. But for that, it is necessary to have a great abstraction capacity, that's why I think that in this profession, the experience (not in years but project quantity) is important.

Sometimes we find ourselves with a code full of comments, readme.txt files as documentation base, extent diagrams that are impossible to understand, names of classes, functions and totally cryptic variables, everything mixed into an impossible to digest hodgepodge: all of that means a huge no exit labyrinth that impedes the evolution of any software and its comprehension by others. The good news is that we can avoid this and the techniques and habits to avoid creating tangled and hermetic software are easy to apply.

A fundamental mistake of any software author is the belief that we will not remember how we have done things weeks or months after: nothing is further from reality. In my case, I still have not left my daughters in the parked car, but I doubt that in a month I can quickly retake the developed code during an intense work cycle if it does not have enough coherence and clarity.

If we do not worry about it we will actively left big stones on path with which we will stumble day after tomorrow or complicate the life the colleague that will take our job. This "dirty" code will cost more money to develop and maintain, subtracting benefits before rival software. For example, the excessive presence of comments on the code, precisely, reveals that something is not getting solved in a simple and auto descriptive way.

As authors, we can choose to write tangled software or clean and elegant software that even a child can understand... For this reason, precisely, we are authors besides professional developers: our mission is to make the text (code) we write easily comprehensible for ourselves and the other members of the team after a while.

This requires an extra effort on our daily work, and we have to know how to think as "authors" besides developers: we write for others to read (and are most cases, the reader will be one's self when more changes on the project are required).

As well as a writer has techniques and narrative resources

with which penetrate better the reader's mind, programmers count with tools and strategies to make our software more readable, manageable and, definitely, easier to maintain.

We cannot develop software if we do not apply explicitly and implicitly design principles and patterns and practice actively good programming habits for the result to be cleaner and easier. This is a truth we should include into our professional DNA: the technical doubt of not applying them is so high that we cannot assume developing without applying these principles and practices. A code where they are not recognizable is a beginner's code, not a professional's code.

However, it is also true that we have to distinguish between a rapid application prototype, a concept test or a minimum viable product of an application that, we know from the beginning, is going to have a long life cycle. In the first case, we can take some licenses to advance more quickly, in the second; things have to be thought always keeping in mind that long term in which the application will continue to be evolved.

Inside the agile development world, S.O.L.I.D principles are considered very good practices on which to base our solutions, the reason? Because their correct application depends of us being capable of generate maintainable and testable code. The correct application of S.O.L.I.D is an art by itself, for which I recommend doing little sample programs where each one of them is applied until we understand them completely or at least know how to read software developed by expert hands.

On the other hand, almost everybody knows or has studied at their academic stage design patterns, but few apply them on a daily basis (they are even implicit on many frameworks that we use): class factory, adapter pattern, singleton, façade, observer and a long etcetera.

There's a long bibliography on how to apply all of these patterns with the more common languages.

Why is it important to know them and apply them? Because with them:

- ✓ Save time.
- ✓ Use a common language so other developers can understand too.
- ✓ Applicate a better and more professional design.
- ✓ Solve common and recurrent problems.

Contrary to what some people think, these good design practices are not looking forward to the making of an academic software, not much less; everyone has received certain information while we were studying about patterns, but few have really count them in when facing a problem.

This is not a technical book (at least not excessively), but what I limit myself to indicate here is that there exist techniques that allow us to crate clean, evolvable code, plus they are easy to apply. I would dare to consider creating clean code more important to our profession than dominating a 100% of language and technology.

As well as learning new ways to do anything, surely correcting previous errors, the application of these design principles will make us modify our way of "thinking" when it's time to solve usual problems: we should do a major abstraction effort; this only happens at the beginning; soon we should have incorporated it as a habit and well-doing will come along. I think it is important to insist on this: if there is any little effort to do to try to learn and incorporate these new habits it will feel like so at the beginning, then we will make profit of it.

I propose you one thing if you do not know this field: each week, study and analyze a design principle or pattern. In a few months you will notice big changes in your way of approaching software and programming.

To get an idea, the application I inherited and that I was commenting on the beginning of the chapter, is still working amazingly, had the following problems:

✓ Extraordinarily big classes and even hundreds of code lines were habitual (this demonstrate little functional separation). This is a typical symptom of an application with design deficit: functions or classes with hundreds of lines...

✓ It made intensive use of cryptic method names and variables, like _pta, _idc, and that sort of stuff (lack of legibility: what complicates reading and understanding any code).

✓ It was intuited that there were functions that apparently did exactly the same (duplicated functionality: more unnecessary code and lack of enough distraction).

✓ The decoupling between the different system modules was exaggeratedly high (this impeded to prove something independently and made it impossible to modify anything without collateral damage).

✓ I could not identify any kind of design pattern (what evidences the lack of good habits).

✓ I read classes and more classes and still couldn't finish understanding the relation between them (lack of clarity in their definition).

✓ User's interface was incredibly attached to all the modules of the application (what caused that to prove something you had to start the application and make various clicks until reaching the exact debugging point).

✓ And, of course, there was not a single automatized test...

Yes, it is easy to judge a posteriori work done by your partners; we must also see the conditions they had to make that application, because sometimes is not a matter of lack of information nor experience; pressure to finish in time, lack of resources, etc. are important influencing factors too.

Do we realize that these kinds of problems are outsiders to

the particular technology used? The same errors can be committed on C#, PHP, Java, JavaScript, etc. Well, it is like that at least 99% of the time. Let's say that non object oriented languages tend to corrupt the solution when it starts to thrive; even this depends on how the developers structuralize it.

Even functioning correctly, it is evident that the solution could have been made with much better quality. The time that was not put in improving the design and creating automatized tests that supported the application was surely seen as a "cost" at that moment; nonetheless, that extra cost goes back to the project with a boomerang effect when the client asks for a revision a year later and the revision costs double, triple o more than focusing the project more professionally. Again, bread for today, hunger for tomorrow...

This is the typical scenery where an application can only be maintained and evolved by the same developer that made it. What I am about to say may sound surprising, but there's people who believes that doing something complicated "intentionally" will make them indispensable: big mistake, nothing further from reality. In fact, there is a chapter in The Black Book of the Programmer dedicated exclusively to this particular topic which is very frequent and harmful to the ones that do this.

Much to my regret I spent many weeks trying to create the environment where the application could function until I discovered that it had been left fixed in the code (what we call hard-coded), in a recondite place of it, an IP direction where allegedly a jBoss server should be "listening" with the correspondent java beans displayed. Later, I localized some passwords also fixed. Can you imagine the uncertainty and desperation after having to spend hours and hours looking for this kind of stuff among hundreds of code lines? Is that productive work? It could have been simply avoided.

Notwithstanding all of that and paradoxically, the clients that had acquired the system were relatively satisfied with its functioning and with reason, or is it that we analyze how a car's mechanism is built before buying it? And I am no talking about any clients: of the good functioning of the system depended the client company winning or losing a lot of money.

The result of this kind of toy software, not professional at all, is that the new expected functionality could hardly be included and we wasted a lot of time (as well as money) forcing the entry what scarcely could be well done or maybe I wasn't sagacious enough to get with the application soon...

The principles, design patterns and good practices are not a passing fashion or complex resources of academics that like to complicate developers' lives, but they are the savior table that will allow us to write elegant code that, later, we or anyone that inherits the system or part of it will understand it with facility. I hope that it has become clear to you with this chapter.

I am surprised by the time quantity that we dedicate to learn new technologies in form of new environments, new languages, etc. and the little we dedicate to polish our skills in the application and comprehension of principles and patterns that will turn our software into a solid building. When we barely know something, we pass on to the next one, and the other, and the other, without wanting to actually reach true mastery and experience on something concrete. Maybe that would explain why it is so hard to find well planned and structured projects. I mean, do you know anyone that has more than five years programming with the same technology? If so, the usual thing is that we tend to always do the same stuff the same way we know, by pure inertia.

I got to recognize that this experience that I resumed here happened at a time when I was not capable of appreciating this kind of things; even knowing some good practices, at this moment, I did not even judged the application as bad: simply, I was the one who had a problem because I could not make it work in time. With time and more experience I started to intuit that the problem was not so much me but the work of the authors that made the application that seem to have been made deliberately convoluted and unintelligible (I mean, it is not about sending a rocket to the moon either); right now when I think about it my conclusion is that that software was not professional at all even when it was made by a great enterprise.

A good developer should be capable of generating elegant solutions from the application of well identified principles and patterns in addition to good architecture practices. No more. From there a "design attempt" will be generated and others will get it easily taking a look at its code. In order to learn to sum we should know the numbers first, just as that, we can only program correctly and professionally if our tools are design principles that we apply coherently in the application.

By last, there is an extended myth according to which the more complicated the more sophisticated software is, surely in many cases it has not been able to simplify things enough. In my opinion, genius consists in knowing how to find a simple and absorbable solution to something very complex.

Key points_

✓ The genius of a piece of code that solves something is that it has been known to find a solution as simple as possible.

✓ Keeping in mind a good refactoring habit allows us to find more simple and elegant solutions each time.

✓ It is not about searching "yes or yes" a simple solution: is that it has more readability and would allow a better maintenance and evolution for the project, saving costs and making it more profitable.

✓ If we want to maintain our friends, there's nothing better than permitting that they inherit well done and understandable software, on the contrary, it may appear people that hates us to death...

✓ Sometimes there is a comments excess (which is not documentation), revealing that the programmer (author) has the necessity of explaining something that isn't evident enough in the code. Some time it is necessary, but not always.

*A turn to the law of change_*

In The Black Book of the Programmer we talk about and insist on the nature of the Law of Change that affects our activity in a very special way: the probability that our software has to evolve and change increases the longer its lie is. This is and imperturbable law and it is weird that someone has not proven it and suffered it in their own skin. It is one of the fundamental premises of agile software, where we also insist in that we cannot know beforehand what changes are going to be executed.

As a developer who tries to do his job as best as possible, I am convinced that the majority of the problems with which we stumble over and over again come from the fact we still haven't digested the mutable and changing nature of any software we implement. There are many reasons why an exploitation solution has and should change, among them:

- ✓ Bugs apparition.
- ✓ A new functionalities requirement from the client.

✓ Adaptation to new legal normative.

✓ The evolution of the market to which the software belongs (electric, online selling, stock market, financial market, etc.).

✓ If it is an international product, specific adaptations have to be done according to the local idiosyncrasy.

✓ The more successful a project is the more changes it needs.

Can we imagine the same Facebook of years ago? Sometimes this level of changes and adaptations is made on a vertiginous way; in the Android world it is talked about the "fragmentation" of their API, which is quite high when they produce a new version every few months. This in itself is not bad, because presumably every new release implements more and better functionality and solves the problems of the previous one. We got to highlight that "change is continuous" here, hence it is necessary in a competitive economy.

Precisely, the continuous delivery (2) concept is fundamentally based on this: coming up with something, improve it and evolve it continuously, but for that software must be improved and evolved with a relative facility.

In fact, on the last few years an ancient concept has been rescued and is at hand for anyone, it is nothing more than DevOps, or what the same is, everything affecting the company's organization, the development and IT team for a fast and continued display of the application's actualizations.

Even when the dominant business inertia is working once and profiting to the maximum the generated product (which I do not say is wrong or anything); on software, things don't work necessarily like that: when a new product is released to the market, the more success it has the more changes and improvements are going to be requested from it. Thereby, the necessity of applying changes could be a success symptom. If so, our software's capacity, if it is able to be improved, will guarantee future success.

You don't have to be very clever to notice that the necessity of being able to modify and evolve our software should be the cornerstone of our developments: according to the agile manifesto, change is always welcomed (12), I would say it is even indispensable for the success of a global economy in which survives the one presents the greatest capacity of adaptation (change).

Nonetheless, as developers we do not realize that this adaptability dynamic is also shown by all that libraries, third-party components and extern modules that we use and about which we build our applications; this fact has many consequences on the life and development of our applications.

Just as the engine of a car would not work if it was not accompanied of the rest of the components of a vehicle, when we develop a new application we do it over the already-made work of others, this is because software has a kind of a "pyramidal nature", we use frameworks, libraries, modules, APIs based on web services or REST, online services and a long etcetera until reaching the same extern construction that constitutes the operative system where our software is executed.

Without going further, since 2013 I am responsible of a product for the electric market called IRIS Teleagement Platform, currently located in Spain and Portugal as well as in Panama and Chile (and the list keeps getting longer); in there we use plenty of extern libraries (logging, task planner, dependency injection, files' compression on zip format, a library to generate excel files, web components framework, a very popular JavaScript library and I am pretty sure that I must be forgetting some). This way, we get the functionality we must implement assembling and using functional components developed by people that we will never personally meet, but from whose we expect to have the warranty of its good functioning and stability.

Thus the capacity of developing software is also about correctly assembling and integrating heterogeneous modules.

Unless we commit one of the beginner's errors that consist on thinking that it is faster to do it one's self than the effort of learning to use an already develop component, this eclectic nature is common of any software professional and is precisely one of the key points that make technology evolve so fast: we like to share and on the key of our business is in the evolution and adaptation of new markets and necessities; our job is very interdependent of other developers' work.

In fact, I would dare to affirm that is grater the effort we dedicate to learn how to use all that component's constellation, frameworks and libraries that orbit around our application than the effort we need to learn a programming language or a particular technology.

I have proven it once again at a MVP that I launched on 2016 made with Node: www.greenkiwigames.com, where I use more third-party modules than I can remember.

It is here comes one of the biggest problems (and mistakes) that the developers have with our applications (and managing teams): if it is true that our software should and has to evolve and change, this component's constellation that we logically use will change too, the "law of change" also applies to those because they still are software artifacts.

The nature of the relation that associates our software with the one of the extern modules we used may seem evident but it is not: on many occasions we find ourselves ballasted by the third-party software's evolution that we chose without thinking it much. Nothing worse than proving that a module you use appears as deprecated.

Should we use the last extern library's actualization when many errors and vulnerabilities have been detected? Logically, yes. But on occasions this represents a big cost because we have to consider actualizing the library and at the same time make sure that all the system keeps on working correctly. One time I saw how an extern component was being so slightly actualized that it started to give a lot of production problems: it simply had not been read carefully that a certain function was deprecated and obsolete in the new version...

It is one of the biggest errors that we commit when we try to decide which libraries to use in our application. The circumstance occurs that we do not know how to adequately evaluate the suitability of a component or other and sometimes we get influenced by the particular tastes of the moment or its current popularity.

I am afraid of those JavaScript frameworks that evolve so fast: it is hard to take a decision with them in a commercial application.

Other times the impulse to use new things "yes or yes" is what makes us take wrong decisions with results that are mid-term catastrophic.

It is common sense realizing that if our software has to be prepared and ready to be modify, the libraries and third-party extern components should too. Do we think about this when we select them? Do we take on consideration the adaptation cost and the new releases of these components on a mid-term?

We can affirm with almost no margin of error that the more popular a library is the more it should evolve over time, which is good, but very bad if our software that's based on it does not do it at the same rate. So, is created a dependency degree that can even put in danger the functioning and correct execution of our project.

A professional developer must center their efforts implementing a functional code, starting quality functionalities for the client. For that, they must use well known third-party libraries, documented and stables, but always making an exhaustive analysis of the suitability of its use in the context of the developing system.

Many catastrophic errors can be committed by a bad choice when we discover that an extern component we used has stopped being maintained and supported, which is something that can happen even if it belongs to a big consolidated company or was maintained by a group of developers in an altruistic way for the community. The risk is the same. What is important here and that I want to emphasize is that we must consider those risks. The responsible of products, like I am, should know this very well.

This situation happened to me when on a website based on Drupal I decided to use a very interesting module that worked acceptably well but was abandoned in short time, when I went to actualize the site months later, there were incompatibilities between this module and more recent versions of others, this forced me to do many changes in the web: many time dedicated to restructure and delete the obsolete module instead of dedicated to give value to the solution.

It is not more than a real example (and I must say that I love Drupal) although this happens on many different contexts. It happened to me at Green Kiwi Games with the Node versions and those from Angular and I know it will happen many more times, but it is natural.

We can see here the two counterweights of the balance: modules that evolve (and improve) fast, which is good, indicate dynamism and that they are used by the community, but at the same time cause traumatism when one is abandoned and presents conflicts with others.

Before choosing a third-party library, we must ask ourselves some fundamental questions if we do not want to plant the seed of future problems:

✓ Does it count with a community wide enough?

✓ Is it a relatively new library and, therefore, predictable of a rapid evolution?

✓ Can I substitute it easily for an equivalent?

✓ Is there enough documentation, forums and community that allow me to use it easily?

✓ Have the new releases respected the compatibility or are they too disruptive?

We cannot advance in professional software if when we chose the components about which we are going to construct our application we do not analyze these terms: the mid-term cost of a bad election could be very high. I am talking about cost, that is, dollars, euros, hard and cold money.

The gravest case I know is about a system, like a very big system, where it was decided very lightly to use Microsoft technologies (Silverlight and Workflow Foundation) that at the time were still a little green and almost right out of the oven.

A year later a new version of these technologies was launched and the adaptation costs were huge (there was no backward compatibility). Not only that but the cloud wave came along and by force the system had to be displayed on a cloud; frustration was complete and absolute and the problems were even bigger when it was discovered that at that time that particular technology was no compatible with Azure, the computation platform of Microsoft's cloud. Again this is another painful but real example of what could happen when some decisions and elections are taken lightly without considering the consequences in the medium and long term. The sad part is that the criteria to choose that technology were more emotional than technical and professional.

The main error that many novice developers commit is using libraries or technologies just because they like it, nothing else. The professional developer chooses them given all the previous considerations and foreseeing as far as possible the possible life time and evolution of the application developing, because on the contrary, it will incur in a risk and a cost for the company.

I am afraid that there are times when we influence ourselves by passing fashion without deeply evaluating the consequences. If we are professionals, we should be aware of the tendencies but justifying or not their suitability to the project in which we are currently working.

Following this narrative we can say that we can talk about "planned obsolescence" (3) when we talk about software: whether we want it or not, the life time of most of the applications is limited. We can (and we should) strive very hard to be good clean coders in everything it represents: design, codification, principles application, good practices and habits. The result will be the notorious elongation of the life time, profitability and exploitation of the system even though it won't last forever because the market and economy will turn around in a few years.

Is ingenuous to think that the libraries and components in which our software is based will remain intact in the next two years (I would dare to say that even in the next months); maybe some of them have disappeared in five years or have been abandoned (is what I call the co-maintainers-wanted effect). I'm afraid there are few exceptions to this.

The more recent and incipient the technology we use is the more that increases the probability of this scenery happening. We do not like at all this axiom of our profession and some may say that they are against of it being that way, even though sometimes we confuse desire with truth.

Logically, we are not going back to the COBOL world or ANSI C either, but always the midterm is in virtue: at any technology or third-party libraries election and components we should evaluate the consequences in a medium and long term.

Even choosing correctly the components to use according to the project's nature, we should always consider some anticipatory and preventive measurements. We have to isolate functionality that some component gives us always thinking about the possibility of its substitution. For that we have to know concepts like dependency injection, interface segregation principle and making sure that the elements of the application are highly decoupled, even if it's at the level of system architecture.

In the recent years it is spoken and implemented increasingly more systems based on architectures with micro services (4). Among other things, a micro service permits decoupling part of the system so it could be easily replaced. By definition, a micro service should be able to be implemented from zero in a few weeks. It is a tactic to avoid the dependency that we talked about on this chapter.

Once more, we know that developing a software application is not only about writing code but we have to take into account some considerations and risks for its life mid to long-term, which could affect the design.

Key points_

✓ The longer our application's life is expected to be, the more it should evolve and be modified (Law of Change).

✓ This law is even more intense for component and extern libraries, because if it grants more specific functionality they become more versatile for evolving.

✓ The more popular and used a library is, the more susceptible it will be to change and generate a bigger number of versions.

✓ The selection of a component or another should not be guided by passing fashion or because it is being talked about by everyone: we have to take an objective decision adapted to the real and future necessities of our application, even though it may suppose the use of "ancient" components.

✓ Those third-party components we use as support for our applications could die, become obsolete or stop being maintained.

✓ We should isolate to the maximum the functionality of these libraries in our system abstracting its functionality through interfaces, using dependency injection or even creating a decoupled architecture.

*Daring to delete the implemented_*

We can imagine a painter who is commissioned a painting with brief and vague descriptions: the client does not exactly know what to ask for. In a first approach, the author creates an outline, a simple draft and after a while shows it to the client. This one rectifies, gives new instructions and tunes some details in which they never set a single thought. In this second row the author has a better idea about what to draw. Starts doing it and taking a new canvas realizes a second approach to the idea that the client has. After showing the result, the client starts to indicate new instructions: they are getting closer to the desired work of art. In this third occasion the author completes on a third canvas the painting that he was asked for: nothing to do with that far-off draft that he first outlined.

Developing software has a similar dynamic with the fundamental difference that when we write code, when we solve a problem the client has, we don't have to throw away canvas after canvas and start from zero; in the majority of occasions we get to the best solution incrementally over what was previously implemented, which almost always requires of a destruction exercise.

One of the main principles of software is that any solution, system, module, library, etc. "increases in complexity" naturally. Well, because over time new characteristic have been introduced or because the initial design did not fit perfectly with the evolving of the solution; in both cases the result tends to be the same: what had a pristine design necessarily deteriorates over time; what started off perfectly ends up degenerating in a certain way when we built more and more functionality over it. This is what happens even when it is our responsibility to prevent it.

This natural deteriorating tendency (software rot (5)) exists equally when we approach our solutions by phases or work sprints. When we go back to a system's section to modify its behavior or add characteristics we end up doing it at the expense of turning it into something more complex.

Over time, this complexity grows and ends up generating deteriorated software, hard to understand and evolve and even worst, practically impossible to maintain. A main rule of professional software is that we have to allow dedicating less effort on maintenance than to incorporate new better characteristics (6); the thing is how to get that ideal world in which the cost of maintaining a system in production is lower than developing new functionality over it.

I have seen on many occasions that some projects had to

be thrown away (and started again) because they had grown too disordered and without a mid-term prevision.

It is natural that this occurs and I doubt that there is someone with some years of experience that has not had this kind of situations at least once. Even more, in some cases, into the obstinacy of continuing on a chaotic, tangled application, it would be the circumstance that if time and maintaining cost were evaluated, they would come to the conclusion that it would have been cheaper to implement them again.

Nonetheless, let's see who tries a sincerity exercise telling their boss that is better to throw away what has been made until then (even if it is less expensive than trying to evolve it). It does not stop being a bit paradoxical and, also, it is hard to explain someone who knows nothing about developing why in some occasions, a software project that has grown during certain time has become impossible to maintain.

If it is natural for an application to grow on complexity "if we do not do anything", it is natural too that the tests that support it on size, number and, again, even on complexity. It is interesting to see how it is not acknowledged that we have to take care of the tests' quality, because it will determine that we have more or less problems when we have to keep on evolving the solution. Personally, I have found myself some time asking myself stuff like "puff, if I simplify this this way, I would have to change all of these tests". The correct decision is doing it if it will improve the system in any way.

In this book I insist that a professional programmer has written in their DNA that it is impossible to develop software without the test backup, and there's an important detail about that: have we notice that we should also make them maintainable, readable and simple? In the same way our solution could turn into something so convoluted over time, so will the tests that support it.

Over the last few years I have proven myself one of the reasons why my partner's code (and my own) has become more complex over time and it is no other than our tendency of not wanting to delete and modify profoundly code sections that at their time we took for closed and completed: definitively, there's an "emotional" reason that impedes eliminating stuff that took us hours of effort to make.

Who has not suffered some time that uneasiness having to delete a class about which they had been working a long time? Don't we obstinate ourselves sometimes in maintaining something about the code intact for the reason that we gave birth to it ourselves? Who doesn't feel laziness improving tests?

It is the same sensation of the painter when their canvases with their first and second attempts of a perfect painting or the writer's they have to undo their book's first draft: definitively it feels like the effort of doing all of that concept tests was not worth it. Nonetheless, we are not aware enough that precisely for the effort of those first attempts we reach a better final solution, be a book, a painting or a software project. Nothing is perfect from the beginning, but we continue improving it increasingly as we better know the nature of the problem.

When we do tests, we are programming and advancing on the solution, and we do the same when we modify something to improve it, even when we delete a code piece to build a better solution.

A professional software developer do not hesitate in deleting whatever is needed as long as it is going to be substituted by a better idea that adds simplicity, better design or a better readability to the solution. It can be claimed that doing this incurs in a time and effort extra, but precisely it is simplifying and bettering that we are multiplying   development's speed: we laid the foundations to be more productive tomorrow, even though this is hard to transmit to our managers.

Unless we have years of experience in a particular sector, must of us have known deeply a certain domain only when we have been working on it for quite a long time. Could someone perfectly implement a communication protocol the first time they have to manage devices at that level? A web based graphic interface made for some users will have nothing to do with its design when it has to scale to thousands of concurrent users. Any data-centric application at the beginning will not foresee each and every one of the reports that the client needs when the project has been delivered. Can accountability system foresee normative changes? Your first web interface is very likely to be worse than the second, and the third, etc.

We could give some examples, although each one has this in common and should be clear by now: software evolves and becomes more complex over time, and because of that, in order of maintaining its readability and maintainability we have to continuously modify the solution (which implies deleting obsolete code sections). I am afraid that many of the disasters on software projects are often produced by not understanding this.

Happens of software that we deepen on the solution that we ought to deliver precisely when we are implementing them: just as the painter's example at the beginning of the chapter, the second and the third deliveries will be closer to what the client really wishes, therefore, how can we think that all of what was first implement has to remain intact on the following stages? Precisely, the agile movement defends software construction as something incremental.

There are occasions when we sincere ourselves completely and get to the conclusion that such library of module cannot be improved in any way to encompass the new requested changes: the next step is deleting them to start all over. This is an honesty exercise that will redound on our work's quality.

There is a word to indicate that something has been completely renovated: revamp. It is precisely used to add value to a new version. This renovation cannot be done without deeply modifying the above, which necessarily implies the elimination or modification of the work that's already done and that worked correctly according to the previous expectations.

I love when I read on the release notes that a new version of a module or library, that they are "fully revamped", that is, that it has been rebuilt from zero to improve it.

Sometimes our own prejudices make us approach software as a construction work in which we produce things: the more we produce, the better, for this reason we also struggle taking that "step back" when we have to delete something. This step back is just apparent, because it is an important factor to take three steps forward.

How do we explain to the boss or manager that we have to completely stake out a part of the application? Surely, must of us have had this problem, which ends up with us dragging modules that should have been deleted for not being honest with our superiors and indicate they had to be substituted. What we lack of here is the other part of the story: what do we get with this destruction act? We always have to tell the responsible what we are getting with the changes.

Personally, I have never worked on any project that did not have to be modified deeply even after the delivery. My worst experiences come precisely from professional time when I was not mentally prepared to throw away important (and unmaintainable) parts of the system in which I was working at the time. Now I know that the most productive thing (on time and cost) should have been completely rewriting those parts from zero.

By the way, this same chapter has suffered that "creative destruction" many times, so it has nothing to do with the original and first attempt to write about these concepts.

Key points_

✓ Software is going to be modified to a greater or lesser extent throughout its life cycle.

✓ Since it is going to evolve, it has to count on a design and implementation as simple and efficient as possible, following design principles and good practices. Design will also evolve, so it is not the best idea to create a fix structure on the architecture and the design at the beginning of the project, not knowing how it will evolve.

✓ Any new change will imply the modification of existing code, and not only adding new functionality, unless we have implemented very well concepts such as control inversion or dependency inversion (11) or some functionality extension mechanism.

✓ If nothing is done, the accumulation of a modification after the other will generate a complex and every time more tangled code.

*When incorporating more people leads to a disaster_*

Once upon a time... I was participating on a relatively important project on an international level, a system of tele management and data management called Titanium (I chose the name myself). As it usually happens, it started off with few resources: we were four programmers without any experience in this kind of projects who had to handle: design, deployments, data bases, costumer meetings, etc.

Time was passing and logically it raised the pressure to have some vital functionality on very tight dates. The project, if well did not posed great challenges, it was economically important because the residual part was the software that gave coverage to the display of thousands of devices in the field, which was economic and main part of the project. If the software did not work well, everything else was in danger.

When a project starts underestimating in resources it will hardly end well, as evidenced during those months. The directive capes were increasingly worried, insisting on knowing the advances' scope almost daily with eternal improvised meetings that take away the thing we had the less at that moment: time to work! I still do not understand why those improvised meetings are allowed or why someone can interrupt you with an endless telephone call. We are usually very respectful of our own time, but don't care for the others'.

The little organization that we managed to have (often working on weekends) was gradually diluting as pressure increased. We lived on a completely hostile project's environment, not because we perceived aggressiveness in anyone but because we were very nervous and we found ourselves very far from getting that relative "peace of mind" that a developer needs to achieve a good design and a good product: the disaster was almost assured. Against some beliefs, an application's design is on daily and incremental construction, each time we decide how to solve the functionality that is being added to the system, no matter how small, for that, we need some kind of calmness and an environment that allows concentration.

The objective in that international project had long ceased to lay the foundations of a great product for the company but get to deliver "something" as it on the dates that the others had committed to without consulting with the people that would had to develop the solution. It is possible that the client requested that dates; however, one way or another, what was committed was excessive for the time we had. Also, we were soon moving to a country very different from ours and, therefore, we were going to get through many changes personally that would affect our daily life too.

Then the unavoidable epiphany moment arrived for the director division (for whom, by the way, I keep a great affection). One afternoon he called me to his office and the preoccupation signs in his face were evident. I doubt that he could even imagine the demoralization, stress and burnout syndrome that we were going through all those who were attempting to advance on the solution. He also had his own pressures. When you reach this point it is not weird that the responsible of the responsible of the responsible..., anyway, the higher the level it is more likely that this question comes: how many "more" developers do you need?

This is one of the more pernicious damages of our profession in critic situations, trying to incorporate more programmers in an advanced moment or at the end of a project when crisis and tension are tangible. And I say pernicious because when you get asked that question you get into a dilemma: on one hand, if you say that it is not good idea then you'll be on the crosshairs when the project twists unavoidably later (why did you not accept more people on the team?, they'll ask), but if you accept to include more programmers in that moment all you do is worsen things.

If we include new member on the development team when we cannot cope with the delivery dates, we are notably aggravating the situation and we will just advance even more the fiasco.

Even on normal situations, including a new member on the team has its "cost" and impact for all the group, in the sense that some part of the time will be dedicated training him about how to work, the project's details, solving doubts and questions (all the natural and logical things we need to know when we face something new).

One of the software's maxima is that to have optimum productivity, a project is started and finished by the same team. That is the desirable. If there's variability in its members then we will interfere on a greater or lesser extent on the natural progress of the project. Nothing worse than a high work rotation of personal at any fairly complex task we approach.

Years later, I was responsible of the maintenance of the same system displayed on one of those "important" clients, for whose work three people were needed because it was on continuous evolution with new requests. Maybe it has been the project in which I've been involved the longest time. Some time I counted even twelve different developers that had intervened at some time; since that there never was a clear leader who took care of its organization, twelve developers meant twelve ways to do things, so some parts of the system had turned into an untenable potpourri. That is the extreme case of what happens when rotation on the same project is high. The system did function, yes, but it had to be feed daily so everything was well, its maintenance was very expensive and, in this way, it was not a successfully made project.

It happens more in software more than in any other profession that even delivering a working solution, according to the time it had had to be developed, the quality of the delivered could be very disparate: if times had been very tight, this initial time "saving" will pass the bill by the major effort that will be required later when it is in its maintenance phase. This is like a constant on nature, almost unavoidable and we insist a lot on it throughout The Black Book of the Programmer.

Trying to incorporate more developers on crisis situations when the most important responsible of a company do not know deeply software nature: we go back to the conception that if a team of two people does a "x" work then four should have the equivalent efficiency to do "2x", therefore the double of programmers will take only half of the time... the part of the story missing here is that the new team members need some time to adapt and also they will take away dedication and effort from the rest of the team precisely at a moment in which there is no time. Sometimes this even costs to be understood by the programmers itself.

There are occasions when a programmer is forced by the circumstances to do a bad job; this is one of them. The background of all of those situations is often the same: total lack of a minimum prevision and organization. But, can we do anything about it? A professional should anticipate to those situations and warn about them conveniently, even though their responsible does not have knowledge enough about those circumstances. If we see that the team does not arrive, before the glass overflows, we should warn whoever corresponds.

It is true that sometimes companies are forced to sell with impossible dates by the laws of ferocious competence of the market, but in the end this competitive advantage ends up becoming extreme pressure to the development teams that won't do anything more than surviving trying to reach the dates "at any cost". It could be understood, but we also ought to understand that a professional developer will not do an equally professional work with this kind of business dynamics.

Doing quality software requires many, let's say, environmental conditions. It is often said that in order to get the best out of people you have to pose challenges that you know they can assume, without overpassing their true capacities and applying, a little bit, just a little bit of pressure to keep the effort and motivation's flame alive. Nevertheless, the problem we are talking about happens when challenges that are impossible to fulfill are asked with an exaggerated pressure. I have seen it, I have suffered it, and I have read many similar cases and the end is always the same: personal disasters and failed projects.

A good developer cannot do a boog job if he is not accompanied and surrounded by certain extern day-by-day conditions; his manager and responsible is in charge of stablishing those circumstances, not him. The downside of the story is that when the project is twisted, it is usually point to the last link in the chain, which is when looking for responsibilities the same developers are complained about because of not having advanced at a better rate. I always say the when a team fails a project, whatever the reason, the responsible is always and without exceptions the leader or manager of the team, simple as that.

We are professional as we get to (and are permitted to) do professional works. Participating on beforehand failed projects due to lack of resources or hostile working teams, only gets us to burn uselessly and to not advance professionally.

It's been ten years since my days working at Titanium (the project of which I was talking about at the beginning of the chapter) and it has rained a lot to me since. In 2012 I started a new professional adventure in which I directed the development of a similar product but for other telemetry technologies. I had time (a year to create a first marketable version), I had resources (a 5-people team), and we assembled an office in which we have an enviable environment, at least for me. Also, I had more years of experience, of course... the result? We developed a product with a great design and very maintainable and extensible, that is called IRIS Tele Management Platform. While Titanium was a project by and for the client, a Swedish utility called Vattenfall AB, almost impossible to install for other clients, IRIS is a product that is being installed by plenty of client with different necessities, both inside and outside Spain.

Key points_

When we find ourselves on a similar situation to what was descripted in this chapter we should consider the following:

✓ The situation will worsen when new developers are included on the final stages of the project.

✓ It is convenient to warn our responsible with enough anticipation that it will be impossible to reach the committed (by others) dates.

✓ It should be noted that there is any possibility of reaching the dates it would be at the expense of doing a less professional work.

MANY PROJECTS FAIL FOR LACK OF ORGANIZATION

It is surprising the amount of projects that end up badly, are not delivered or are thrown away not because of deficiencies in the technical skills of the working team, but because of a nefarious organization and a complete lack of planning.

*When a project's manager becomes your worst enemy_*

I got to recognize that I have suffered many bad experiences with nefarious project managers, to the point that I started to intuit the huge importance of counting with a development team with a clear and professional role that correctly executes that role.

At any work group every piece is essential; it is not about assigning a major importance to who has the more responsibility, but about realizing that each member of the team needs of the others and these as well need him so a common project goes forward with aspirations of quality and success pretended. It is like this at any collective project in which the result depends of the good collaboration of all of its members. I am afraid that not all managers, coordinators or agents, understand it this way. Especially, some have their special idiosyncrasy.

Whether we like it or not, on most of the companies with development teams exists a person responsible of its coordination. Notwithstanding, I think that many projects end up in disaster because of the simple reason of counting with a manager that has not done a good job or well, "does not fit" into the responsibility.

In other occasions, the excellency of the development team is the perfect front of the manager's wrong doing, in this chapter we are going to dedicate to the first case, because a bad development team responsible could suppose the worst risk for products and solutions that could be better and more successful.

The number one rule for a manager is that he has to know to some extent the nature of software development; we cannot coordinate the creation of something whose details we scarcely know. This seems evident although in some occasions we find people in this role that has no idea of what to do and how does the product evolve.

Who takes relevant decisions about a project ought to know what is software development, how does it evolve, what are the real risks that some decisions carry and how does the selected methodology affects the process. It is not weird to find managers with none or null experience in this sense, especially at big companies where exists a high intern rotation and people can go from a place to the other "rebounding", promoted or hand-picked without any meritocracy in between.

A director of a car factory must know the special nature of vehicle fabrication, a greenhouse owner must know how to manage it from the most basic; a write must generally know the edition's process of his own books and in the same way, the responsible of a software development project has to know to a certain extent how to build an application and be familiarized with its fundamental concepts. I am not saying that they have to know every detail about how all of the involved people does things, it would be impossible, but they must have an overview of the whole.

They don't even have to be experts on some of the technologies they use (their election could be delegated on someone more expert in the group) but they must understand the main aspects of good software.

If it is not like that, how will a developer indicate the necessity of improving (refactoring) some modules if the manager does not understand that we will increase the work's speed that way later? Does he knows about the technical doubt of not having a project supported with unitary tests, of integration and validation to guarantee the system's correct functioning as changes are introduced? Simpler still, does he understand the huge difficulty that supposes to even estimate a concrete task and that any assessment we do will always be an approximation more or less real?

A manager is obliged to know profoundly the methodology implemented. This may sound as truism although I think about a certain project in which the stand-up meetings (7) ended up during more than one hour (everyday!). How can anyone pretend to maintain methodologic discipline of a work group if it is not profoundly known?

We are talking about a team's responsible that works directly with the developers and, therefore, must know all the circumstances affecting negatively or positively their work; knowing these circumstances is their role and responsibility, since the result of the common work will depend directly of it.

An essential component is that a manager knows that developing software, even considering it logically a work as many others, has a continuous artistic and creative component and requires of some calmness so the developers work fluidly and concentrated. A developer takes design decisions constantly and cannot guard down when it is time to generate quality tests.

I firmly believe that a professional programmer always tries to do his job as good as possible, even though he needs some "peace of mind" because of the elements I was commenting earlier. The manager is the responsible of generating this peace of mind in the team and create the necessary environment to make a good job, it seem like when we talk that relative appeasement that we must have most of the time we are talking about something mystical, nothing further from reality: a software developer needs some daily calmness and certainty so the work does not get affected. Actually, any person that realizes any creative task needs them. Essentially, this supposes not suffering constant interruptions, that you get invited to unplanned endless meetings, get continuously asked to do some tasks for before yesterday, etc. An environment that is free of all of those elements is almost impossible, but it would be enough if at least 80-90% of the time the developer could work concentrated and focused on his work.

A development team that works under stress is going to necessarily produce a worse result than the one from a good creative environment. Productivity is also this, achieving better results simply by having a better work environment.

Effectively, they pay us the same salary for producing something, but no one should lie to their selves because circumstances determine the quality of what we produce. We do not live in an ideal world and as human and emotional beings that we are; we suffer many factors that make us face the creative work we do one way or another.

Sometimes the manager projects his own anxieties, pressures and uncertainties on the team he manages: a good manager never does this, he must "stop the blows" before they reach the team and distinguish who has to carry what and when. It is not about trying to live inside a bubble isolated from the rest of the things that happen in the company, but about impeding that some elements affect unnecessarily and negatively the development team, especially if those elements are other roles' responsibility.

One time I worked in a group in which the responsible

was in and out the department, precisely because of the bad results we were getting; this example is not about finding the responsible for that situation but about indicating the bad environment and anxiety that existed in the group because that manager transmitted all of his insecurities to each and every one of the team members. This situation lasted some months and I got to recognize that at an environment like that it is impossible to try to do the best work possible when you are waiting for the clock to mark the hour to go home.

One of the biggest vices of bad managers is not complying with was planned (if the plan does exists) and decide at will someone's task content from one moment to the other, especially when changes or "unpredicted" requests appear making the programmers team work bouncing from one thing to the other with a total lack of prevision. Nothing worse for a programmer than changing context continuously leaving unfinished tasks: returning to them requires of an extra effort that, of course, is totally unproductive. One of the principles of agile development is that done means done (13): we start a task and we close it "completely"; this increases productivity at several levels.

What happens is that productivity does not get along with inefficient team managers.

We are no longer talking about lack of clear requirements, something almost natural on software, but about of these changing so often that make the tiniest organization. It may be extern scenery, although the manager ought to know to say "no" to his own superiors or to the client himself when the situation is unsustainable. On many occasions, this improvised way of working has behind years of inertia or simply a total absence of someone who marks the way of working.

Obviousness related to the equipment and tools we work with: programmers do not do a paper-pen work (well, sometimes we do, but as a mean to start proposals with draws, schemes, etc.); we usually need hardware equipment dimensioned enough and tailored to the kind of project we are working on. Much to my regret, I have had many experiences in which it came to the point that compiling a complete solution delayed more than five minutes at my work station. This is really frustrating; dead ties could be counted by hours throughout a simple week.

On another occasion proving a solution was extraordinarily complex because of the security rules of the company's web. How many hours lost for that kind of problems!

In complex environments, they surely need more equipment to test deployment when not a sufficient system if we have implemented a continuous integration environment.

Everything resumes with the most common sense that a development team needs adequate means to work. The responsible is who has to detect those necessities and proportionate them, noting more. A team's good productivity is determined by counting with the hardware, tools, connections, etc. necessary so the work is made fluidly and with the minimum obstacles; the team manager most reduce them as much as possible.

And I am afraid I can tell many anecdotes... during my step by some "big" company I had to continuously connect to a VPN of some foreign client. To do it we had to make authentic pirouettes from our computer because of corporate "security restrictions", or at least that's what we were told every time we tried to change the situation. The result was a very uncomfortable, slow and cumbersome environment to solve problems with the client. This productivity loss had to translate necessarily onto extra costs and a worse quality result (and a boring technician).

Any work that has to be done in person, if we expect to do it right, needs of a minimum organization and planning; if we have a team of people to make that work, in order of making it fluid correctly, this organization must be even better and if, also, the team is multidisciplinary with differenced roles, not finding a correct planning may cause chaos.

You have heard that before, don't you?

Many of the project's managers that I have worked with did not know how to organize and plan correctly; this is my traumatic experience and I would like to think that it happens differently in other places. On many projects, we probably could have done a way better work (and in less time) if we had had a better organization "from the top". I always say the same: when extra hours stop being punctual to become something chronic and the modus operandi of the day-by-day, there is almost likely, bad organization and planning behind.

So that a programmers' team works productively enough (which is not working more but better) it needs to function like a perfect gears machine: this organization must be provided by the responsible, but for that we must work hard organizing and planning, not "arranging".

Even when everything is always improvable, my current responsibility consists on managing all the software development division of the company; I dedicate approximately between a 20% or 30% of me time to organize the team and plan the evolution of the products we are developing. I would like to think that the good rate at which we progress and the quality we are getting has to do precisely with that time I dedicate which is the major responsibility of a project manager: organizing and planning. I hope to succeed at this effort.

"Managing" means deeply knowing what happens in the working group, how are we going to take decisions if we do not know the real progress, the day-by-day problems and the vicissitudes of the group of professional that work to obtain a good result? And for that there are many different styles and methods...

Asking is good, even when many software project

managers ask so much that they are constantly annoying the rest of the team or well they are used to convene spontaneous meetings just to resolve their own doubts; that is the attitude of someone who thinks that the team is "below" him, even because of a bad hierarchy understanding, when it is actually the manager who has to be at the service of the team so it could work in the best conditions.

Organizing is also dividing the complex on easier tasks. Any considerably complex work has to be simplified while having control of the adequate tools; a software project manager must also count with tools that show him how everything is doing at any moment without being continuously asking or calling. If you do not have any kind of management tools (there being, also, some that are free with enough quality), without that how are we going to detect important deviations, etc.? If we do not have all of the relevant information while during the management of a project in some authorized way, we cannot anticipate to the problems. A manager must anticipate them and work to minimize them; for that he must use the adequate tools.

I got a lot of experience using Visual Studio Online Services from where all the team has visibility to the tasks, working sprint definitions, the backlog items catalog or user histories, etc. also, in the market there are plenty of tool equally valid. The important things is basing work on them and not resorting to excel or daily mails avalanches...

Now well, what happens with the developers? We cannot have right without duties the same way we cannot demand everything done: we also have the responsibility of favoring the duty of the responsible. Developers should also permit correct fluidity on the others' work; the manager is just another member, no more or less important, but if he is present, then we should favor his work with the transparency and honesty that characterizes a good professional. There is nothing worse for a working team than a "troll" who continuously boycotts others' efficiency. This is also a problem that must be solved.

Many projects fail loudly because of the ineptitude, lack of professionality or knowledge of who is responsible of managing the team. Software programmers rarely live at isolated environments, but they belong to a group with which they have to coordinate. The better the group functions, each and every one of its members, the better we can do our job and the better the global result will be.

If a software project fails on any way that we understand as failure, the main responsible of it is the manager; no need to review it again. Precisely his work is to move pieces, generate circumstances and detect obstacles so the common project ends up successfully.

Key points_

The activity of a bad manager can be easily detected; in The Black Book of the Programmer we center on all those aspects that negatively affect the development of good software; we could say that the quality product is directly proportional to the well doing of the manager who directed it. A bad manager:

- ✓ Does not implement clear organization and planning.
- ✓ Allows or provokes unpredicted tasks very frequently, when it should be something very punctual.
- ✓ Does not impose any kind of project management tools (or well what he uses is a spreadsheet...).
- ✓ Convenes spontaneous meeting as a usual working mode. I am not against any unpredicted meeting if the reasons are urgent, but I am if they are summoned constantly.
- ✓ Creates uncertainty and anxiety on the development team by translating personal inquietudes.
- ✓ Does not know the development methodology used. A bad project manager "thinks" that it is not one of his functions.
- ✓ Is incapable of maintaining the required methodologic "discipline" in all the artifacts that must be generated. Nothing worse than skipping methodology on a crisis.
- ✓ Does not worry about improving the "group environment" nor detects "rotten apples" that should not be there.
- ✓ Accepts any radical requirements change and planning modifications without any opposition.

✓ Does not detaches enough authority (not "authoritarianism") so people respects his decisions.

*The daily life of a good programmer_*

Like on many other professions, some of the worst defects we can commit when we create software solutions may be inconstancy: we know that what we have in hands must be finished due to certain date that looks very distant at first, so when we start it is too much the temptation of working very relaxed. This also applies to personal projects: if we do not commit to finish stuff with a calendar more or less clear, everything will remain as a useless attempt.

As time goes by we realize that we accumulated many tasks and we star to work harder and with more dedication. Soon appears burden, rushes and extra hours, at the same time, the quality of the work we carry out starts to suffer, the tests are stopped and the methodology is left aside.

For the record, I am the first to fall into the temptation of this way of working on many occasions, although that is also why I have been able to analyze the long-term consequences on productivity, personal satisfaction and the validity of the work done.

This lack of discipline and constancy has different results when you dedicate yourself to another kind of activities: the one that fabricates screws will end up fabricating less, the one that repairs vehicles will have to spend more hours on the customer's bill, the one who paints a villa (for example) will take longer to finish the job increasing the probability of winning a dissatisfied customer. In that kind of jobs per hour the unavoidable will be that you lose money because you have delayed more delivering a product be screws, be a repaired vehicle or your neighbor's house painted and shining. Any work made on the rush is always worse, and it should not be anyone's surprise; however, I have the sensation that people is always rushing on everything they do, having the need of it or not. There is an oriental maxim that I do not doubt of its pure wisdom because I have years applying it: less is more. To get to the objective, the best constancy is quality, the persistence of the natural impulse.

However, on software, this lack of constancy affects radically the intern quality of the developed work; the product will surely function (even though the probability of delivering it with errors increases), but must of the capital sins of software would have been committed and they will pass us the bill later in the form of numerous "to do's..." not implemented, pending tests, spaghetti code, etc.

Work inconstancy on a programmer is paid with an increase of the technical debt (everything we left and ends up exploiting later, to us or to a partner).

A good software developer works with discipline since day one. An ingenuous mind with little experience will think that this means working hard and intensely at every moment. This discipline will not make you work more, on the contrary. Working with order you work on a relaxed mood, assuring the quality of what you are doing and reaching the planned dates with commodity. This way of focusing work adjusts to the creative nature of software and, also, since software development is incremental, you are advancing on solid and firm pillars.

I have seen it (and suffered) over and over again and I must say again that it is a mistake to think that who spends more hours (or who spends more time in the office) is the one who works the most, when actually this should be interpreted precisely as a lack of productivity and day-by-day inefficiency symptom. This lack of productivity could be organizational or personal.

We must notice that since we suppose that a professional always wants to do his job as good as possible, other organization and planning problems could interfere. Another matter is that software development cannot be measured by hours, but by results. This is of course a very wide subject, but we could conclude that when someone continuously "needs" to spend more hours of the workday to finish their tasks, then we are in front of some kind of organizational problem.

In our curriculum we do not mention at any moment the

laws that follow good software development: we do not advance in our work better when we dedicate intense and discontinuous development cycles but when we are capable of maintaining a relative constancy and enough creative intensity at all times. We already know that stress and pressure go against the programmer's good habits; therefore the tactic will be to avoid them as much as possible.

We can resume with an example the most important habits on the day-by-day of a good developer: we have two weeks ahead to implement a solution and what we have to do is perfectly defined, there are no doubts about it. Notwithstanding, there are some gaps about how to implement some parts.

A good developer identifies the main pieces of the solution, starting to approach to that thing that he "still does not know" how to implement or how to shape, this is, we start with that thing that bothers us the most. This is fundamental: if we finish first what disturbs us the most, we will rapidly delete the mental purr of having even more uncomfortable and hard things to do.

We make a prototype to prove the best way to do this or that. When we have it, we are ready to integrate it to the general solution. Then we are completely calm because we have already solved what bothered us the most about the development. This way we resolve the hard part first and accumulate it on the last days of the two weeks when other problems will be overwhelming us.

One of the solution parts is made and validated with tests, unitary, integrative, etc. we will not talk about whether we use TDD or not (test driven development), this is not a technical book, but if we left constancy that we have to test the module or part we are working on to guarantee that, later, when the solution advances and evolves, that particular part still functions. Moreover, we have to automatize those tests so they could be executed over and over again: definitely, they will show you that everything you have done functions correctly.

You keep going with a second module where you start to see some similarities with the first: you do not duplicate it, but you spend an hour to see what those similarities are and extract common functionality: you abstract something previously unpredicted. This requires effort and surely touching the first module. Modifying it, you will also have to change some things of their tests. Here we hit one of our biggest defects: the apprehension to modify what we know it works, as we already commented carefully in another chapter of The Black Book of the Programmer. It is not retouched just because, but to "improve the whole solution"; therefore, we are investing time and effort on something that will have its benefits later.

We finish the second module and before starting with the third (it already happened the first week), now that we know how to solve the solution, we ask ourselves what of what has already been developed that we could improve or simplify.

This is a fundamental question, because if we include it in our professional developers DNA, what we are actually implanting is a continuous betterment to our work: we build things bottom up. Improving on something these first two modules will report us benefits from now on.

It is surprising sometimes the little time we need to simplify and improve something. There are times when it is just a matter of minutes: when we realize we can do something better at the same time we read some inconsequential tweets (for example) then we will have taken a level jump. It is very frequent that the big betterments of a solution are not caused by a big structure stake out, an organizational one, etc. but by the gradual accumulation of tiny incremental improvements.

Going back to our example, once we had done the change, how are we sure that the modules are still functioning? Thanks to the fact that we have supported everything with tests of the development we have already done, we execute them again and check if everything still functions correctly. Surely this last simplification probably made us change and improve some tests; this job is not an expense but an inversion, because with it we guarantee the functioning of our solution and we have a method to check if it still works just as more functionality is introduced.

Then we face the third module, with the discipline of a constant work and the recurrent question "can I improve or modify anything?" and with the discipline of continuously executing tests to quickly detect unpredicted bugs.

It happens to me sometimes that I suffer of a continuous mental purr when there is something I should do at some time of the week, for example, but is something a little bit tedious, humdrum or is simply a problem that I have been dragging but that has to be solved. Without realizing it, there are continuous alarms popping up inside your mind like "you got to do this and that thing you don't like at all". Finally, comes the time when I decide to do it and to my surprise, that something that was chasing me for a long time is liquidated in a breath. Then, I always ask myself, why did I not do it before and "get it off"?

Without realizing it, our job is marked by those little insidious tasks we have to do whether we like it or not, if they are done quickly, it is better to finish them off soon and avoid your mind continuous alarms, so we dedicate ourselves with calm to the rest of the things.

An advice proposed by David Allen on his wonderful book "Getting Things Done" in which he describes the working organization method GTD, posing that whenever there is something that could be solved in less than two minutes, it should get done instantly. Avoiding mental ramblings continuously reminding us that we have something to do; those ramblings impede us to concentrate in what really matters.

This continuous work process we described before, although very simplified, is what allows us to get to the end of the second week with the finished work and the safety and satisfaction that we arrived on time showing that what we have done functions correctly because it is properly supported by tests and with a huge internal satisfaction for having done a good job. On the book "The Passionate Programmer" (8) by Chad Fowler, it is referred the necessity of finding that happy satisfaction in our job, to which, by the way, we dedicate more time than anything else on our day-by-day; therefore, why are we accustomed to waste that much time of our life on something that will "only" give us a salary? We have the obligation of looking for a satisfactory activity and try to be happy with what we do; personally, I can say that one of my biggest satisfactions is see finished a good job.

This creative process is interrupted or impossible to do if we do not maintain that minimum daily discipline, that constant look back that allows us to identify what to improve and what to simplify.

The day-by-day work should always consist of constancy that allows us to build solid solution parts. If we rush, the first thing we will lose will be the so necessary tests to check if everything functions correctly as we introduce changes, if we let time go by and start working hard on the last days before the delivery we are risking ourselves to crash and surely what is done quickly and badly will have to be redone later (bread for today, hunger for tomorrow).

Recently, while I was writing this, I faced the development

of something completely new in a three weeks sprint: on the third little of what I had done on the first remained untouched, the tests had nothing to do with the ones I did during the first ten days, the design had emerged naturally and finally I had a solution with the guarantee that it worked (at least it got through all the tests) and the satisfaction and desire to keep evolving it.

Honestly, are we comfortable when we have to retouch a brittle solution that breaks at the smallest change or new requirement? It is more likely that we could and want to evolve elegant, well designed, clear and simple software.

Do we understand that that discipline we talk about makes us get to the second stage? Definitively, working that way, more organized and in a good mood will allow us to enjoy tomorrow out work as software developers.

Key points_

✓ We should always start a work phase with the most complicated part; when we suppress this preoccupation, we will face the rest of the tasks more easily.

✓ We have to be constant with the solution's progress: nothing worse for software quality than alternating intense work cycles with others of inactivity.

✓ A good developer always "looks back": searching into what has been already implemented something to abstract, improve or simplify. This way, we learn the best way to build a solution... building it!

*Talent, Technology and Methodology_*

Some time ago I was asked to evaluate the state of a software project, a mix of ERP, CRM, etc. The client, in this case, the owner and manager of the company, wanted to know the advance level of the intern development team responsible of it.

The preoccupation was evident: they passed the scheduled dates and did not have the nerve to see something that would allow him to suppose that he was making progress in a project that, in short, the client was financing and that was going to be vital for the future development of the company.

This is one of the big problems of our profession: the incapacity and difficulty to indicate clear delivery dates (this is, that the client knows when the work is going to be finished).

Meanwhile, the development team was reluctant to show anything and was not even capable of offering an estimated date to deliver the solution. I wonder if "delivering" or not something finished and closed has any sense on software.

The frustration and restlessness of the first was proportional to the team's uncertainty: a very complicated situation, tense and unpleasant for everyone involved.

It took one hour of talking with the solution's responsible to detect some endemic evils of our profession. Twenty minutes of looking at the code were enough to find out many "you ought to" that cried out to the heaven; I needed even less time to make some conclusions after seeing the "evidences" that the developing team had left on the project's management tool. Too many similarities with other projects in which I had participated. Why do so many people always run into the same stones?

After this experience, I have been hired many times as a software quality consultor, and I have found similar situations where the client wanted to know, generally, why his solution could not advance faster and what did it needed to acquire quality. The black Book of the Programmer is a two-hundred answer for that question.

I do not find pleasing at all when I am evaluating the work of a partner who makes a living doing the same as you, with more or less success; presupposing the good will and disposition toward the job, it is uncomfortable to detect (and communicate) the insufficiencies and shortcomings. From the base that everyone does what they can and on many occasions we are not given enough necessary conditions to advance in the proposed work correctly and with quality.

The case I was commenting at the beginning of the

chapter is just one more but, nonetheless, is paradigmatic on a big amount of projects: most of those who fail do so because they have an unbalanced combination of talent, technology and methodology. But, what do we understand by these three concepts for the success of a project?

You do not need to be no guru (have I already said that gurus or "machines" of computation almost never sever to work on a development team?), nor a star of those who when they are hired say that they have-signed-up.

The success on the achievement of a software project, more or less complex, involves a development team with differenced roles, it is not a single determined factor, but in several and those have to be equilibrated enough.

Some team members could be great, even brilliant and deploy talent everywhere; they like everything they do just as investigating new ways to do and improve what already works. They cause the "wow, I would have never thought about it myself" effect; they go so fast in their way of causing astonishment that they do not have time to document what they do (why if it is already great?), they also do not like nobody to put up on them several "post-it's" with the tasks they should do for the next days because that could restrict their creativity. When they read an article with an amazing work that I call "plumbing-enginery", they quickly feel the necessity to apply it to what they have in hands at the moment "in whatever way", even forcing it. They are, let's say, flawed by their own genius, they deploy an overwhelming talent but you cannot ask them to be centered, stick to the established standards and give visibility of what they're doing at all times to their manager, boss, scrum master or whatever. Their genius and skill makes them unpredictable and work in an improvised way.

On the other hand, other team members go at a pace, let's say, less accelerated, and they struggle more to understand what they have to do, they blunder very often and proactivity is a very complex word for them. They do what they can, always supervised by someone so they cannot be asked to do many inventions or to have more initiative.

Those are opposing sides of "talent". I always assume that people are smarter than they seem and there are true rough diamonds that not even then can suspect they are. The lack of talent does not coincide in a loss of intellectual resources... but in a lack of motivation, attitude, working satisfaction, etc.

This is not a coaching book, but I must point out that, like at any other activity, programming with motivation gives better results than programming without it, something evident that everyone should notice.

On the other hand, some team members have an amazing technology domain: they just need to see the symptom of a problem to detect where the cause is, they know what plumbing work to do to achieve a result, they like that the-more-intricate-and-internal-the-better stuff.

Instead, there are others that just google whenever they

have to implement an abstract class and do not know why does the compiler protest, they search in forums that new message from the IDE that tells them that there are circular dependencies or before the problem of "listing the List <> in alphabetical order" they search in the Internet how to "show alphabetically a List<>". They are, definitively, woke people, but without a doubt, for "other kind of stuff". No need to confuse talent with it but with knowing well enough the tools, frameworks, architecture, life cycle, etc. that is used on a project.

It is useless to have talent and know all the details of the tools and technologies if we do not have an organized framework that allows us to advance with the team.

This is a key point and is synthetize in the following question: have you decided to follow a methodology in the development of the solution? If the answer is "yes", then comes the second, is that methodology really followed with the same intensity and strength throughout the life of the project? Now, the subject itself of using or not a methodology has substance and content for a separate book...

This is like the collectibles after summer or the well-meaning proposes at the beginning of the year: desires and wishes are often confused with reality, since we boast about following this or that methodology but we don't recognize that we started off nicely, then we slack and when we have the littlest time pressure or let ourselves be guided by indolence, the first thing we abandon is methodology.

We talk long and hard about this in The Black Book of the Programmer, but let me remind you that a very subtle reality exists only within reach of the initiated: when pressure appears on a software project, the first thing that dies is methodology, it's the first victim, but surely the lack of methodology is what caused the pressure in the first place! Understanding this requires some introspective effort when projects fail and we have to analyze the cause of these failures.

Implanting a methodology without the discipline of applying it every day is not following it, simple as that. Sometimes I've been more interested in saying and publicize that "we follow this or that methodology" rather than actually apply it with all its consequences.

Thus, we see that there are three concepts to apply to our software developments, now we are going to ask ourselves how we fit into each one of them:

✓ Do we have talent? Or, people perceive that we have talent for what we do?

✓ Do we dominate the technology which has been decided to use?

✓ The manager of the project counts with discipline to implant methodology with the same strength at the beginning, during and at the end of the project?

✓ Do we gird ourselves to that methodology at all times

in our role?

✓ Do we count with enough formation and resources to use the project's technology well enough?

We will see the answers to these questions, starting from sincerity, they will give us a "yes, yes, of course this and that, but not that", or "well, that documenting thing..." or "my thing is codifying, I enter a fluidity state and time flies, but those project control meeting kill me, to me, they are a waste of time", and a long corollary of possible combinations.

A project's failure is always determined by a bad combination of those three concepts: talent, technology and methodology; or what is the same, a project's success always counts on these three factors well balances, but the three at once and with no absence of any of them.

This takes years to realize and what is worse; it is hardly taken into consideration by the management teams when it comes to organizing a new project. One of the main fails of a manager is unknowing the strength or weakness of those three aspects inside the team he is managing.

To resume it a little bit: it is useless to have a radiant and natural talent solving software problems if we do not dominate well enough the subjacent technology we use, little we do knowing all the tools and frameworks used if we do not have the discipline to follow a methodology defined throughout the project and also, it does not matter how much methodologic discipline we have if we are not capable of doing a flawless software module.

What happen in the case I was talking about at the beginning, that project that I was asked to evaluate?

On that regrettable case, the three pillars of success of a software project failed: talent was not insufficient, shaped as a team without the necessary experience on a similar project (I am not saying they were dumb, not much less, they were and are very smart and competent people), the domain of the technology used was improvable (in that case .NET framework and related technologies, Entity Framework, etc.) and, to top, the project was strongly started following scrum but it started to dilute little by little (after a few weeks), not clearly perceiving the methodologic profitability of applying it with discipline.

The result of all that was not only a failed project and a frustrated team that really do not finishes to understand what went wrong and that has actually worked with the best will in the world, also there is an economic gap the someone has to cover.

Key points_

✓ Many software projects fail because there wasn't the correct equilibrium between talent, technology and methodology.

✓ In my humble experience, and after many years working on projects and creating products, a lot of talent and technology knowledge is available and almost always what fails is the correct implantation of a methodology, whatever this is.

✓ It is preferable to have a good combination of those three aspects than counting on those "gurus" or egotistical lone rangers incapable of working in a team. Our profession, I do not know why, maybe because of a media and childish image about everything related to computation and those super-cool hackers, is full of excessive egos. Stay away from them.

✓ The team's responsible most evaluate those three factors and detect strengths and weaknesses (even though I recognize that this is always much easier to say than to do).

The software architect's misunderstood role_

There was a time when I participated on an international project with a wide group of developers implicated; the professional skills of those was unbeatable, we all wanted to face new challenges and also (unusual thing) we even had a group of testers from the beginning.

In the Black Book of the Programmer we center in those things we do wrong as developers and the reasons (almost always the same) why projects fail. This time, I am afraid that the presence of a software's-super-architect is going to be described more as an obstacle than an indispensable role.

Well, the project I was talking about failed loudly in a few months: eventually we were able to make work what could have been a magnificent product although for many it turned into a real nightmare and a really bitter work stage.

Among the many errors committed, the main one, to me at least, was clearly establishing someone with the role of "architect" so parting from his design and architecture decisions the software universe that should constitute the project and the common success of the group was developed.

I am afraid none of that ever happened, fundamentally because of a bad conception of what was an architect. It came to a point where implementing a new functionality was really hard because we had to solve it with an inadequate software architecture. This was wrongly stated as something closed and was also established "at the beginning of the project"; even when the requirements were still not clear and we did not know we were going to solve the ones we actually knew. This way, all functionality had to be embedded as it was in that architecture.

But, what do we understand as architecture in a project?

When we program we are continuously taking design decisions that are related to the rest of the components of the system (new methods on the API-rest that make us restructure it, new consults to the data base, a new class or module to avoid duplicity, betterments on the message mechanism of the log of the application, etc.).

On the other hand, architecture, whatever it is, the classic client-server, of three-levels, etc. it is not established just because, but depends on the next two factors:

✓ The type and nature of the project that we have to solve, something that seems evident, but I am afraid that I have seen architectures applied to projects where they did not fit at all.

✓ The life a project will have, this is, if it is going to be evolved over many years, if it's going to be closed and never modified again, etc.

✓ To my understanding, a person can perform that role as long as they have at least the following conditions:

✓ Has a high experience for a determined "domain". This is no one can be considered a "software architect" for any kind of project. Good developing involves knowing the kind of business for which we develop a solution.

✓ Has gone through many roles throughout his career (tester, developer, analyst, etc.). This means many years of experience with different profiles. Nobody ends their academic formation and quickly become a "software architect"

✓ Has worked on many kinds of projects.

✓ Not only must he have total control of the technologies used, but he also has the ability to decide which are the best ones for the nature of the project: a software architect does not say "we use java net beans because, because I like it and period" or "we are going to use the last .NET framework because ... it is the last of the last". Maybe this kind of decisions should be made by the technical leader, but putting our feet on the ground and in reality, we see that this kind of things (architecture, technologies, how and why) are almost always decided by the same person.

✓ A software architect must also know how to lead and guide the work of a group of developers. In theory we can see this role as that of someone who writes brainy documents, but in practice, if it exists, it is only one of us who makes decisions (and should be responsible for them, of course). In addition, a grassroots developer needs to know the reasons for design decisions that he himself has not made. Nothing worse than programming in a boxed way inside architecture without knowing it sufficiently.

In my opinion very few people have a profile with these characteristics, among other things is even weird to know anyone that has more than ten or fifteen years programming, given the frivolous cultural business according to which ascending means managing leaving aside technical matter..., a problem that we have talked plenty about in this book.

Another reason why it is hard to have a profile like that is due to the vocational character of our profession: if you really have years and years improving and developing frameworks, projects and products is because you really love what you do. How many people I have known that abandons the art of programming after a few years for other, let's say, simpler activities. Software development is perhaps one of the professions that force you the most to reinvent yourself continuously given the enormous and rapid evolution of technologies, uses, tools, types of products, etc. As a result of all this, few remain at the bottom of the canyon for many years.

I support in this book, and I also say it and I affirm with perfect knowledge of cause and experience that in most projects the role of a software architect is not necessary: to speak of such a profile is as much as saying the cascade development model is still the example to follow.

I may be wrong but at this stage of our profession it's been demonstrated that posing an extraordinarily closed architecture "at the beginning" of a project is a deep and big mistake. I insist in what "most projects", because on those projects in which multiple agents intervene like, for example, diverse companies with different responsibilities, it is necessary to establish how are the diverse pieces of the puzzle going to fit.

It is necessary to pose some general lines, but being those open enough to admit change later.

On the other hand, we must not confuse the architect role with the responsible or technical leader, even though on many occasions they may be the same person.

Unless you have a much dilated experience, when we develop software we completely ignore how to solve some aspects of the solution until we really have the problem in front of us and we have to get ahead anyway.

Other times, what we thought was going to be a walk of roses at first turns into a Calvary due to the amount of unpredicted problems. We often misunderstood the requirements, especially those badly taken, other times the requirements are on excel and they are also obsolete...

We are precisely defining the kind of problems that surge when we understand software development as something predictable when, on the contrary, it is more unpredictable than we thought. Hence the need for another type of scope when solving software problems.

And then agile development appeared...

There are so many uncertainties when it is time to program something that the only possible scope is doing it little by little. Instead of delivering a completely finished solution at the end (which will be probably incomplete according to the client's expectations), deliveries should be short and frequent, making sure that we are advancing at a good pace.

Agile development consists basically on that and all its methodologic variants.

One of the characteristics I like the most about the agile is that design and architecture of the system surge ("emerge") as we advance on the development itself.

On centering on the exclusive development of a part or functionality of the system we realize that the application's architecture is not something that should be thought about sensibly at the beginning, but it surges spontaneously as we implement little by little the established requirements.

Logically, advancing that way forces us to implement code in a different way: we prepare what we develop so it is easy to modify and change, include functionality making sure at all times that the previous does not stop working and, especially, doing continuous refactoring.

There is an abundant bibliography about agile development and it is not a matter of extending in this chapter about something that today should be part of the cultural heritage of any professional programmer, but suffice it to say that by focusing development in this way, the role of software architect is diluted; it is, shall we say, more dispensable.

The "forced" presence of a software architect who makes us bind the solution to an architecture designed at the beginning is more an obstacle than a positive element in the project. I have proven (and suffered) how on some projects the developers work more and dedicate more time to forcibly fit something into the established architecture than doing useful software. This problem is very hard to solve because is precisely the presence of a software-super-architect what reveals the existence of hierarchized roles: a total obstacle to the democratic and horizontal development of a project.

This does not mean that once we have the requirements we have to start developing like crazy, quite the opposite: in the middle term is where the best decisions always reside. A certain type of general elastic architecture as a development framework for the solution must be established, but for this it does not need a role so closed that it occupies 100% of a person's work.

And I am afraid that it is a matter of ego too... in my humble experience, when I have found someone engaging the architect's role failure has been surely back: this role is used more as a power hierarchy into the working group and of social recognition than as a pleasant element in the development of a good project. The truth is that it sounds better to say "I am a software architect" than "I am a programmer", even when the dedication and experience of the second one exceeds in several levels those of the first.

I have also seen how agile development has had many difficulties being established into working groups because it comes with the abolition of some roles that we think about as, let's say, more respectable.

With agile development, architecture emerges as its evolution advances. To some extent, so the software architect's role vanishes. This idea was so revolutionary at the time that I think that only the ones who have seen projects fail due to erroneous design or bad architecture have embraced it completely.

Key points_

✓ Most of the projects do not need the presence of the software architect's role.

✓ It is necessary on very big projects with plenty of agents involved.

✓ Given the working progression of most professional programmers, just a few can reunite the requirements needed to be considered "software architects"

✓ The agile scope dilutes the role of a software architect: architecture emerges by itself as requirements are implemented.

WE MAKE THE SAME MISTAKES OVER AND OVER

Developers have in their hands the responsibility of producing quality software always in the optimal conditions and when we learn proactively from those errors that ballast our work and that productivity is what allows us to be centered in what really matters, what adds value to a solution.

*Methodologic profitability_*

The following is nothing but a fictitious story that we repeat constantly; anyone who has just a few years in the software developer's profession probably has found their selves in this situation more time than they'd like.

"Once upon a time a city commissioned the construction of a skyscraper to dazzle the visitors: inside it important companies would be lodged and even a part of the City Hall's dependencies. Moreover, it had to be very high and aesthetic so it would take part of the city's skyline over time.

The construction company, as soon as they received the order, sent the first crews of workers to the place to clear out the big piece of ground where the emblematic building was going to be. To save some time, the architects of the company partially left their other projects aside (...) to start what it would be their star project from now on.

Building licenses were required at the same time that the

ground was being drilled to start the foundations. The concrete loads were reserved for several months to the local cement companies and before defining the external structure, conversations were already being held with important national and international glassmakers.

After a few months the astonished citizens of the city could see how a concrete structure that grew every day arose almost from nothing. At half a year, the exterior facades were covered with different exterior designs.

The project's first crisis emerged when the surveyors realized that the electric connections were in the wrong places (...), water supplies had not yet been contracted in enough advance and the insulating material did not fit the structure left by the last architect who worked on the project. It was resolved frantically breaking here and there and with some food in a luxurious restaurant with the manager of the water supply company...

The next year, when the weeks for the inauguration were already counted and when the local news media were already mobilized, a placid summer Sunday, a deafening noise made all the alarms jump. The neighbors, terrified, peeked into their balconies and those who walked through the streets saw a huge cloud of dust rising to the sky.

The emblematic building had fallen like a card castle, the work of hundreds of workers, technicians and engineers came down in a matter of minutes: in those moments there were already those who thought of the heads that would *roll over the batter while the city lost its magnificent and iconic building."*

Well, this simple and fictitious story that has neither feet nor head describes how we face software construction most of the times, including big and important companies.

Would someone think it is normal to build a skyscraper in such a way? That disastrous way or working is common for freelancers, small companies and big multinational companies with development departments. Have you heard about it? Only in small islands of clarity and motivated "from within" by the developers themselves, begins the building of software, say, in the right order.

Is there any relationship between the construction of a vehicle, a building, an olive packing machine (for example) and a software product? Yes, a lot: all of those entities have to be developed and have been created in the abstract world by some thinking heads before existing, they are terribly complex and it has been necessary to establish a clear development script for its construction.

We are talking about managing and making works that altogether are not easy, are hard to approach by just one person or working team.

Just as it happens with a movie production (someone writes the script, it is hired, begins the locations and cast searching, the scenes are recorded and then come the realization and commercialization works), anything minimally complicated has to count with an organized structure with clear steps to follow according to the nature of the job to do.

This may look elemental and obvious for "other activities" is not that easily understood when we build relatively complex software and want it to be in the market for several years.

Software does not escape this complexity and, therefore, needs its own waybill taking the risk of ending up like the building from the story because of its absence: translated to our language, this waybill is nothing more than a development methodology.

It is hard to perceive that methodology is not just one thing more to add to the own activities of development, but is an intrinsic part of it: we are always full of work, following this or that methodology is assumed as something more to add to the task list. We are, say, lazy when it comes to assuming and following with discipline an organizational method, whatever it is.

Because, although some believe they do a special job, very technology related and it makes us feel kind of special in a childish way, behind all those fumes we are still humans, unless the Reaper visits us and, therefore, we have the same vices and virtues as the rest of mortals.

It is usually preferred to develop those parts of the system that attract us most and leave the most boring for last, without mentioning other tasks such as generating a correct documentation, deployment guide, integration and quality tests, etc. Sometimes I have had the impression that many developers try to spend most of the time "playing" what they like, ignoring or avoiding all those tasks that do not bring them any kind of fun. In the real world, everything is important for a project to conclude successfully.

Why don't we perceive the necessity of following a methodology the same way nobody thinks to build a building if they do not have a project signed by a master architect and endorsed by the corresponding professional association? By the way, why do construction architects have always a "sir" ahead and computer engineers don't? We will leave those considerations for later...

Jokes aside, we suffer this constant temptation of ignoring methodology due to the intangible nature of software: while you can clearly see walls, windows, plumbing, floor and doors quality, etc. in a building, a client who asks us for a system is barely going to perceive the users interface and, if anything, will notice its stability or instability: what is behind so everything functions correctly is completely ignored, even if it is rotten and about to fall. Just with projects with much business volume and an advanced client I have seen exigency of evidences of the implantation of quality processes, including the correct use of methodology.

On the other hand, we do not see clearly that that building could fall (or will fall with the littlest of changes months later) who it is going to crush in its fall is ourselves or our partners if we are lucky, what leaves much to desire to our professional honesty. A software building that falls to pieces is a problem for who has to lift it again, but it is also a huge problem for the company we worked with for incurring extra costs that could put into danger the balance and viability of it. We are not talking about things with any consequences, they have a lot.

When we build a system without a clear order we are leaving "methodologic profitability" aside, which is nothing more than building well now, at the right time to lay the foundations of the system in its initial stages, following a well-established script to move forward with order, so that once the solution is finished and delivered, the system can be reused , maintained and evolved, multiplying the results, customer satisfaction and our own by working on something well-built and without failures. If we do things right, later we will get that so prized profitability shaped as errors absence, system's evolution capacity, higher earning, a more satisfied client, etc. methodology, of course, is not the only thing needed for that, but it is indispensable.

A professional software developer does not argue or doubts about applying or not a methodology: it is part of his DNA, just as a pharmaceutical does not deliver a drug with no prescription or a constructor does not build a house without an architect's project.

Then, why do we so often leave aside the discipline to implant a methodology throughout all the phases of a project? This will show us when and how to advance on the project: it is the guide telling us how we are doing on the system's progress, how we are team working and which tasks does each one do. Without methodology we will struggle a lot more trying to decipher what functions and what doesn't, we do not know if we are deviating from the objective and scheduled dates or if we are at the adequate pace, we will ignore the stability of what has been built already and we will not have a single way of minimizing the errors of the system.

There's no movie without a script the same way there is not successful quality software without methodology.

The working group's responsible; manager, coordinator or boss is the one who has to demand the presence and following of a methodology: not doing it they are avoiding one of their responsibilities.

The main reason why we elude following an organizational method correctly when it comes to developing software is because we enjoy the freedom of doing something (programming) when and how we want to. This is an ingenuous and candid view of our job; only when we have seen that doing things organized, rigorously and without leaving loose ends, is when we start to truly appreciate the value of working with a methodology. On personal projects, samples, concept test or prototypes it is valid to apply cowboy coding (9) and have fun with it, but on a professional project that we or the company we work to is going to profit, we cannot elude the implantation of a methodology, whatever it is.

Sometimes we overvalue the implantation of any kind of organizational strategy when it comes to doing software. A methodology, no matter how hard the fashion and academic rigors crush us, is nothing more than a set of norms about progressing on software development, the responsibilities of each role and the kind of software artifacts and evidences to be build.

In this order of ideas we have the capacity to adapt any methodology to real necessities or a project's particular structure.

If we support a software product's development under a methodology's umbrella, the appropriate for the project's nature, we will move forward safely and profit its application shaped as a more sustainable code (less errors) and simpler to evolve (adapting times for shorter requirements), among many other advantages.

One of software's laws that I have experienced myself is the effort dedicated to implant and follow a methodology with discipline will redound proportionally in a better technical profitability in the software we develop, this is, if we effort applying the chosen methodology, whatever it is, we will improve the product's quality in the shape of less errors and better maintenance.

Key points_

✓ A professional project must count with some kind of methodology; moreover, it could be defined by a mix of some of the existents as long as it adapts to the nature of the project.

✓ As professional developers, we should always demand its implantation and following.

✓ Supervising the following of a methodology is one of the responsibilities of a working group's manager.

✓ If we move forward correctly on the project, with order and clarity, we will accumulate the "methodologic profitability" from which we, the project, the company and the clients will beneficiate later.

*Everything is in the UI_*

I still keep in the drawer of my working table a CD with all the information, documents and codes of a product in which I worked during my first two years just after finishing my academic stage. I have not thrown it away for pure nostalgia, even though I have to recognize that was the time when I learned how to actually program: those were the times of C++, COM, DCOM, ActiveX, etc., when you could spend entire days trying to detect a slippery memory leak that made a service overflown within a few hours of functioning. It took days to implements things that are a basic part of a higher framework now.

When I thought I finally "knew" how to program, the first edition of "Code Complete" by Steve C. McConnell fell into my hands. It was like some kind of epiphany that made me intuit that there are many types of "doing it even better" and that, also, software quality was a very polyhedral and hard to value subject even by the own professionals. That one CD is capable of sheltering the entire work of a ten-people software development group for two years, hundreds of thousands of code lines, thousands of tests, documents written in Spanish and translated to English, thousands of software artifacts that fit into the palm of a hand.

Here it is one of the main problems software developers have to face: the intangible nature of it makes extremely hard to value the effort dedicated to conceive, design and implement a solution. And there is the result of the work of all these people for so long? , could ask anyone alien to our profession.

Other kind of products somehow project the effort employed to produce them, for example, a vehicle. Nobody imagines just one person designing and building it. It is easy for anyone to think of a big working team that had participated in its development, probably thousands of workers functioning inside a big sized organization. A car, a household appliance, a mobile telephone, any physical thing detaches by itself the effort applied to develop and fabricate it precisely because they are tangible objects, that can be touched, so we intuit the enormous complexity of its mechanisms.

I am afraid it is not the same way with software that, at most, a client could see the user interface, some reports, that some process are executed at enough speed and stuff like that. Complex, yes, but don't "detach" in any way its complex nature. Even less when the tendency is to simplify to the maximum the processes or workflows of the users, with minimalist interfaces thought to do the desired with a few clicks.

The main problem is that since the effort of our work cannot be seen clearly, only those who understand the nature of software development can imagine the effort or dedication necessary to produce an application.

We can value the money necessary to generate the content of the CD I was talking about at first: surely its total cost was superior to half a million euros; the result? A software product that fits in a single and simple CD of several cents ..., impossible to value in "material" terms.

This casualty of software affects us in many ways and we often make the mistake of not reminding it when we approach projects or have to "sell" our work: we underestimate the fact that a client could unfairly rate the effort and dedication necessary to develop something just because they only come to perceive the tip of the iceberg.

But, what can we do about it?

That's right, we can and we should; we are in front of one of the typical problems of our profession: we do not worry too much about showing the value and effort of what we produce and when we do it, sometime we try that the client sees something complex to justify our work, when what he wants from us is to solve his problem easily. I stumbled with this stone many times at the beginning of my professional career.

On the other hand, a new element complicates this matter

even more: we are totally immersed into a paradigm by which by should offer the user easy-to-use applications, like I pointed out before, and at the same time hide the enormous subjacent complexity that they actually have for its functioning, that is why they say user manuals are made to not be read.... We can look for it on Google: completely minimalist user interface, does anyone imagine the terribly complex entrails that must be behind according to the search algorithm apart from the huge hardware infrastructure that permit that everything works so wonderfully fast in a global deployment of the searcher? However, our entry door to it is a text box, a bottom and pretty images that change every once in a while and it all seems to function magically... Everything is perfectly described in the fantastic book I recommend by Steve Krug, called "Don't make me think! A Common sense Approach to Web Usability" (10), even web focused, the elemental principles are the same for any other case.

Offering functionality to the user is the easiest way possible is a usability and design challenge itself and, at the same time and in a paradoxical way, makes it even harder for a third to value justly the necessary effort of all that is behind for it to function correctly. We are in the era of simplicity, in many ways, which is in my opinion good news because it is deeply related to productivity.

We tend to overlook that the main factor that values the quality of our wok is the user interface we are capable of developing and its answer time, this is, the only truly visible thing we can show to the world as a frontage for our application: the only thing we can "see" is therefore the only thing we "perceive". We have it even harder when we pretend to simplify it to the maximum so it would be easy to use. This is a dilemma we will face continuously. It is true that we should value above all how much we improve and the value our solution brings to the client's business, but they frequently obfuscates about it if they think it is ugly, little intuitive and complicated to use.

Like the expression "you don't only have to be good but look like it", on software development we can say that everything is in the UI, or at least almost everything. From the UI a final user can perceive the quality of the software infrastructure that supports it, even when it may seem unfair.

It is true that there are many other factors by which an user or client could value us positively or negatively, like good support, being able to solve problems or incorporating new characteristics quickly, quality documentation (just in case someone reads it), etc., but all of those attributes have already passed the universal filter of an attractive user interface.

We have recently decided to change the graphic libraries or charts we used on the software platform where I currently work. The previous one, although functionally stable, seem a little bland... when changing it for the new one (a payed product called Highcharts, available at www.highcharts.com) and integrating one more feature than the default, we could say that now some graphics appear more visually (with the option of zooming into data blocks, downloading an image from the graphic, etc.). Those are functionalities that the client is not likely to use, however, the impact they do on demos and presentations is, simply, spectacular.

With very little effort we managed to multiply the positive appreciation of our potential clients, being the system's complexity exactly the same.

Not in vain I learned my lesson, since the publication of this book back in 2014 until the second revised edition I have worked on many web content projects (Walkiria, eVision, etc.), I have given a lot of importance to the design of their user interfaces.

I perfectly remember an occasion during a previous working stage. I developed a framework to the management of a type of dispositive which use was very complex (digital tele management counters with PRIME technology). That development simplified the work with them in a way that was much more trivial its integration into applications of higher level. Also a great effort was made to establish a group's structure and methodology sufficient for the scenery in which we were moving (we were all working at the same time in various projects...).

Many hours had been spent on the project when the first

results were presented to the people of the other department who were in charge of commercializing the product. I know that we made a great job, with the conditions we had, and also things functioned relatively well, there were not many technical doubts and the foundations were well established so the development could grow and evolve.

However, the first comment I heard in the presentation was "well, what a s#!t...", what logically made us feel a deep frustration.

Time helps you analyze some situations so when I think about that presentation I now realize that we were the ones who failed: we were so centered on backend, nothing trivial I assure you, that we did not think that it would not be valued enough not even by our intern clients (of the company, if there are) or the extern (the finals). We did not put the necessary emphasis to create a pleasing user interface: it was too plain, with a hideous design and also, hard to use.

The lesson there was clear: we could have developed a wonderful user interface, with a magnificent design and pleasant effects and surely, the impression of the system would have been fantastic, even when internally everything was rotten and badly done. In that occasion, that dumb incident planted the seed of many doubts about the project, so we are talking about stuff that could have a very important impact in our work.

We should not only do a good job, with the foundations of some norms to advance with order (methodology), acquire as habits the activities related to simplifying the design and continuously refactor and, why no, support everything with automatized tests; also we should always show how wonderful everything is with a user interface that is liked by someone who has no idea (and doesn't have to have it) of what is going on internally.

And we have to assume it: the user does not care about how much we suffered to simplify the design, or if we were loyal to the fantastic agile methodology; they don't care either about the number of tests that guarantee us that any new bug introduced is going to be quickly detected. The client will only consider the "value" that it brings to the solution, the time saved by implementing it in some processes, the substantial betterment we bring to their business. The tool they have to perceive all that value is undoubtedly the user interface, at least for most applications. If it fails, the positive appreciation of everything else will plummet.

This is like a law that is fulfilled in software development that we should always keep in mind.

And it is not only a matter of interfaces; the same principle would apply to a wonderful backend whose API was complex to use.

Last, if we do not show how good our work is with those extern attributes, we are making a big mistake that could even put in danger the project's viability. Even more, knowing it works like this, we can use it as a strategic tool:

instead of centering the initial efforts in everything we cannot see (data bases, APIs, backends, services, etc.) what we can see can be prioritized strategically and therefore, valued better.

Key points_

✓ We should dedicate more effort to an agile user interface, easy to use and with a good design. On many occasions we are going to get more profitability due to this aspect than the internal details.

✓ An intern client (of the same company) or extern is never going to value how efficiently we have solved something that is extremely complex.

✓ A product's value has nothing to do by its amazing architecture nor or how sanitized is its code, but by the value and utility that it can bring to the user; for that, in most occasions, the user interface is the toll to our application.

✓ Sadly, sometimes, the progress measurement to our boss or manager is nothing more than "what can be seen" through the user interface and this has to be taken into consideration.

*Technological dilettantism_*

We hear very often that everything related to the Internet and Information Technology goes very fast: in a short time someone can go from being up to date to feeling completely outdated and obsolete. It is true that things are move at a vertiginous speed, and we are not talking about the huge information flow that hits us continuously, but about the forms, uses and new tools that appear competing with each other. Without going any further, everything related to blockchains is every time more present in the media world (blockchains, technology underlying bitcoin), machine learning, artificial intelligence, IoT (internet of things), etc.

In this narrative, any user that habitually uses a computer can feel overwhelmed trying to follow that frenetic rate. It looks like in this scope "being up to date" just means knowing (at least barely) the last news on tools, applications, new devices, etc., even when tis use is the same as ten years again.

This phenomenon, stressful in my opinion, also affects

software developers; let's say we are not just users with tools, applications and work and leisure utilities at popular and domestic reach, we also suffer the same kind of avalanche about the types of technologies used for the development of those same tools, applications and utilities. Let's say we are double bombed by it. Another recent example: everyday more frameworks are published on JavaScript...

In the years I have developing software, almost twenty while I am working on the second edition of this book, I have seen a little bit of everything and surely I have been left with many things; but I still cannot intuit what I have left to see:

✓   On this time I have used five different versions of the IDE environment with which I've been programming 80% of my time. Of the super advanced Visual Studio (that I still use daily), I have gone to use advanced text editor such as Sublime Text for my projects with Node.js.

✓   I have used many versions of control systems (I am talking about Visual Source Safe, Subversion and the code repository of Team Foundation Server). And, of course, GIT, that I use even as a version control tool for documents.

✓   I have gone from using a kind of formal methodology, to another period in which the word methodology did not exist until completely embracing the agile scope of software development.

✓ I have worked with many technologies for user interfaces (MFC, ActiveX, ASP, ASP.NET, ASP.NET MVC, PHP templates, jQuery, JavaScript, JFC/swing, HTML5, Angular, Node, etc.).

✓ I have followed the huge evolution of the programming language I have used the most over the last five years (C#).

✓ I have used many different versions of data base server from the same maker; in terms of databases. In the same way, we have already made a real project with big data technologies (Hadoop through Azure, the computer platform in Microsoft's cloud).

✓ I have seen how concepts like SaaS, IaaS and PaaS are now a reality for any kind of client.

✓ A cloud's computation was a concept too abstract just ten years ago. Now it is to the order of the day and the migration of systems to the cloud, when we did not design specifically for it is great.

If I had been told at the beginning of my career that most of the clients I have in the company uses new products deployed on the cloud and billing in software concept as service (with periodical fees), I would have not believed it. In the same way, from spending a lot of money on books and manuals I started to buy them from my Kindle, as well as subscribing to online services like Packt Publishing (www.packtpub.com) and SitePoint (ww.sitepoint.com), and also doing online courses on many MOOCs, some free and some on reasonable prices.

At this point you probably made your own conclusions: current tools, environments and work forms are going to evolve five years from now. It is like we had to reinvent our profession every once in a while.

A software developer who starts on this profession has to have this clear; there are no comfort zones that last long, unless a few occasions; if you insist with the immobilism and not leave what you know, you will be soon out of the market.

This seems obvious, but it is not so much the tremendous effort in hours of dedication, adaptation, new learning, etc. which is used when jumping from one well-known technology to another. Few professions have a pace of adaptation and evolution as high as software development. We ignore the professional cost that this has in our career.

This change after a dizzying change is a cause of stress in those who discover a few years after disembarking in the world of the company that this characteristic is intrinsic and part of our profession: either you adapt or you die (I mean, you stay in the greater obsolescence, surely losing economic or labor opportunities).

It is also a cause of wanting to escape this dynamic of continuous evolution and adaptation trying to capture management positions, but that is another issue ... I wonder if this is one of the reasons why the number of software developers is decreasing after a certain age. It is rare to find professional programmers over 45 years, at least in Spain, which is a real tragedy for talent when precisely the experience and background are very valuable to make good software products.

We suffer a frenetic evolution (sometimes due to commercial reasons from the Internet's great) on the technologies and tools we use, that is undeniable, but the question is that we on many areas "are still solving the same problems". And so?

However, it could be very tempting and even dangerous hang up to the last fashion, because on software, like on any other industry, exist passing fashions and technologies that seem very promising and then end up disappearing into oblivion after a while. And this happens not because they are good or not: on software something is good if the community or the market adopts it, that's all that matters.

Here is the crux of the matter and the fundamental error that, in my opinion, is what I myself call "technological dilettantes": the development of professional software is sometimes confused with that marathon to be "aware" of the latest of the latest, without having gone deeply into what we have at that moment in our hands.

We forget that we are professional programmers only and exclusively to "solve problems and give utility" to others. The technologies we use for that are not the end itself, but the mean to bring value and create something useful, which brings to my mind one of the agile development principles:

"Working software is the primary measure of progress".

Without falling into the simplicity of criticizing others, I see how they dedicate (and waste) huge amounts of time reading technology and gadget blogs, pecking here and there without going deep on anything, while trying to get out of the way as fast (and unprofessional) as possible in which our actual job demands.

Then why do we like this deluge of news, updates and new ways of working when we already know that most of it will be obsolete in such a short time? Simply because we do not repair enough in the effort we dedicate to that kind of vain gossip instead of creating solutions, innovate with entrepreneurial ideas and solve real problems (which is what gives us food, as they say)

With this critical discourse I do not want to give the idea that we should avoid that frenetic news hurricane, not much less, but highlight that we lose a big part of our effort by trying to follow it. To some extent, professional software developers, should and have to be aware of the last wave (the technological state-of-art, which sounds a bit better), but without forgetting one thing: our effort must be centered in solving problems.

This is another software law that I like to repeat as a mantra: we will only succeed if we know how to use technology, whatever it is, to solve a problem and bring value to someone or to a business, or what is the same, our success possibilities are reduced if we "only" occupy ourselves in knowing more and more technologies without going deep into them and... not solving anything or doing anything useful!

First thing is the problem, and then we choose how and with which technology solve it, not backwards. What gives us prestige as professional are the problems we solve, and secondly how we solved them. I know that there is a tendency on curriculum's presentation to show the projects in which one has worked, and not insisting in the technologies used for that.

If it is true that we are getting closer to a new working paradigm according to which the only thing worth will be what we can bring to an organization and the results, it does not make any sense that we fill our curriculum vitae or our LinkedIn profile with stuff like "Expert programmer, JavaScript, prototype and jQuery since three years ago. Expert on ASP.NET MVC. Medium knowledge of Ruby on Rails. High experience on data bases like SQL Server, MySQL, and MongoDB".

Or well, stuff like ".NET Framework 4.5, WF, WCF, Entity Framework, SQL Server 2014, IIS 8, AppFabric, Team Foundation System, Visual Studio 2015, C#, ASP.NET, Visual Basic, Active Directory, SCRUM, GWT, PaaS: Google App Engine",...

It is not wrong to highlight the technologies we know, but we got to be aware that those things do not say "what we can" do with them.

This is the product of what I call "technologic dilatants", programmers that are surely good professional, technology passionate, with great talent and also have the luck of enjoying knowing new ways and searching here and there. Notwithstanding, I am afraid that we are starting to live in a globalized world in which it is every time easier to hire with a click a well prepared Indian engineer who dominates the same technologies as you.

Then, what can differentiate us competitively? Only the problems we can solve.

A professional software developer can only talk about himself exposing the jobs he has made (the problems he has solved), independently of the technologies he used; definitively, nobody is going to really examine the level we have in each and every one of those subjects we indicated we know in our curriculum, which makes it have the same value as a wet piece of paper.

If we are professionals as we solve problems, then we should expose our great abilities like "Co-founder of a social media for the valuation of quality vines (implemented in X)", "Development with Microsoft technologies of an application for the monitoring of servers", "Design and development of a system for the management of smart meters actually on production of X electricity companies", "Manager of scrum workgroups, Visual Studio Online since three years ago", "Author of the user's guide for X", etc.

Results, results and more results.

Those are the problems we really solve in our day-by-day and have our signature, the only thing we can expose about the quality of our work, nothing worse for the development of a professional career as an expert programmer than falling into an exaggerated technological dilettantism.

Key points_

✓ We are going to be better professionally valued by the works we have done (the problems we have solved) than by saying we know this endless list of technologies, frameworks and ways to do knots... this is a technological version of that saying "we are what we do, not what we say"

✓ It is true that we have and should be aware of what moves (sometimes we are the ones who cause that movement), but this should only consume a little part of our productive time and effort.

✓ Technological dilettantism is more about an ingenuous vanity than actually wanting to know technologies to innovate and solve problems.

✓ It is frustrating to know that many of the technologies we use right now have a planned obsolescence, but this is part of our profession and if we do not digest it well, we will be out of the market early.

A GOOD JOB IS ALWAYS BORN FROM A GOOD ORGANIZATION

This is one of the best kept secrets: we can only achieve good and abundant results if we organize effectively; for that, we should dedicate some of our time to plan the tasks we have for the next weeks and commit with the settled objectives.

*It is not about working more, but working better_*

There are certain realities that overwhelm due to its simplicity: on software, working more hours is not increasing productivity, so nobody is surprised that not to spend more time in our work is going to produce more and with the optimum quality expected.

Sadly, we have all "warmed the chair" sometime during the realization of a project and this is not always bad as long as it is something punctual; it takes part of the culture of working presentism. Now well, when you need to be more hours than the habitual as something chronical there is no doubt that something is not working in the organization, the way of approaching projects or maybe we assumed way more work than we can handle, for example.

Software creation, as an activity with a great part of creative nature, can only surge when the adequate conditions are given to take the best decision at all times. We hardly notice that when we are programming, we are taking design decisions continuously. We are hardly going to guess when we have ten hours of tiredness behind; impossible to refactor that thing you know would come out better when you cannot wait to get out of the office. So, little by little, this kind of conditions happen when technical doubts, that make the final quality of the product or project go down a few steps, start to accumulate. I cannot get tired of repeating it: we are professionals as the quality of what we produce is good or excellent.

Competing producing in quantities and bad quality, in my opinion, has a mid-term run, although I know many companies based their business models with those parameters: hiring a lot and cheap, because then developers will execute projects "at any cost".

Since some years ago I direct development teams and I am, let's say, the "boss" of the office in which I spent a big part of my working time, dedicated to projects and products for the company as well as own (that, in the best scenario, end up generating a new profitable business). What I mean is that I am not talking from the perspective of a broken "employee", but I have the responsibility of a manager who's in charge of the business' development.

Nonetheless, sadly there is some management mentality according to which if an employee fabricates twenty screws per hour, forty at two hours and so it goes, then a software development will produce more working more time. Nothing further from reality. I hope I am being clearly understood: a programmer is not a special breed of employee, not much less, even when some programmers feel a bit special with an arrogance varnish that I, personally, find very annoying. Nevertheless, it is absolutely true that the effort of putting our full attention in the details and in the creativity of design is something we can only keep on doing a few hours a day, let's not talk about a retrospective of what has been done so far in order to face better the future development phases; this affects and much the quality of all the software artifacts we produce.

And so what if the delivered has a worst "internal" quality if it works for the client? I really hope that at this stage of The Black Book of the Programmer that question could be easily answered. That poor internal quality will make the software hard and expensive to maintain and evolve (profiting it even more in the future). This idea is difficult to understand to those who do not "live" software from the inside. It is true that the agile development indicates that the only progress measurement of software is whether it works or not (working software), but we got to qualify that if it is not made with enough design simplicity, code cleanness, good development practices, etc. what we do on subsequent phases will be hard to produce or impossible to make.

How do we get to the situation where we have no choice but to spend more and more hours in the office every day? Whether you work for a "salaried" company or are freelance you can equally suffer the causes that make you work in a totally unproductive way.

Starting a software project with enough resources and time is of the most gratifying moments of our profession: ideas are clear, we know what to do, we got on the table a lot of things to investigate, the opportunity of participating in dojos and doing concept tests before minimally posing the system's structure, looking for frameworks to support on, we can even dedicate some time to evaluate the tools that we are going to use and, sometimes, even decide the best methodology, and all because we have enough time ahead (or at least we think we do). If we do not have a project's manager who is aware of this and who controls and plans the times correctly, the habitual is that we start projects relaxed.

This is a fundamental error in which we all fall before an incipient project. I am afraid that you realize this dynamic when you have already made that mistake and have a few years of experience.

As time goes by we prove that there is a growing sensation that we are not going to arrive to the scheduled dates and, reaching this point is when we start to relax methodology, tests and, definitively, the quality of the development. When we talk about "quality" we are also talking about cost and profitability we can obtain from that software.

Maybe it is due to a responsibility effect or maybe because the responsible starts to tighten the nuts and the workday lengthens dramatically. If we consider that developing software is a creative activity, similar to the artistic one made by and sculptor or painter who is abstracted by their works, then we could see clearly that the creativity state cannot last eight, nine, ten hours a day. Even more: I believe that it cannot even last five. Have you noticed that you past from productive intervals and others where you barely advance during the day?

The end of the story is that some weeks before the delivery is when we take more hours than ever, but they are not completely productive hours but hours when you work at jump of kills to deliver "anything" that allows us to get out of the way; when our minds are invalidated by this objective, the quality ones, betterments, good code coverture, etc. have no place left.

Therefore, even if we reach the committed dates, we will have done things so wrong that we will never apply again the "bread for today, hunger for tomorrow": the price we paid then is lengthening even more the posterior phases of the project (due to software's unsustainability and plenty of undetected errors from not following the methodology correctly if we did not abandon it completely). Then the problem is hard to solve.

We see how parting from the ideal conditions, we end up taking more hours and warming our chairs. When this happens and we see people with their eyes flaring at 8 p.m., we cannot say they are working productively: those hours precisely indicate that things have been incorrectly done since week or months ago.

Perhaps some boss likes to see his employees so "committed" with the company's objectives by continuously staying more and more hours at the office. This could impress and even improve your valuation among "some kind of bosses", but the reality is very different: needing more time of the workday is an undeniable failure, a problem that must be solved and a clear symptom that something is not going right into that organization. Of course, there are employees who like that their bosses "caress their backs" continuously and nothing better than being who turns the lights off and closes the doors of the office last when, maybe, who work better and correctly had already done their job efficiently and went home by five. And also there may be who tries to cover their own deficiencies (and laziness) spending more time at the office, there will be everything, and as project responsible, we must be aware of all those dynamics.

I have always wondered why on many occasions when I participated on a project time has come over us. Now I am very aware of the answer and the bad working and organizational habits that cause this situation. And we must not forget that working long periods with stress and hours excess causes a bad quality result and this is what a good professional should always avoid.

What we are talking about is nothing more than knowing how to work productively, which is the opposite to solve a time crisis dedicating more hours to a work that we are going to make way worse on such conditions.

There are many factors the cause this kind of situations. Up next we will analyze the most common that I have personally suffered at some time.

» We do not know what we have to do with enough anticipation

I remember some years ago I surprised myself realizing on a Sunday night that I did not know what I had to exactly do in the office Monday morning. I only had to go and according to the avalanche of e-mails attending to these or those things depending on its importance, the predisposition I had at the moment or the priority that "others" gave to this or that matter. I had work, a lot, but with a complete absence of organization and clear finish dates. The result of this situation is that we magically had a crisis the next day because "someone" demanded something for the next day. Software was being made, yes, but with no planning and, therefore, I am afraid that the quality of what we developed was not excellent.

» We continuously get non-scheduled tasks

This is one of the clearest symptoms of lack of prevision and planning. It is unavoidable that some subjects appear without us or our manager to remedy it: a client's urgent call, an important offer to listen to, etc. Now well, when unpredicted tasks appear continuously as something usual in the company's way of working, we are in front of a big problem that will make us incapable of planning anything or doing software with enough dedication. The race towards excess hours is served.

» Technical doubts will come back around us often

This happens when we frequently detect that due to not having improved something at the time, a critical refactoring we did not do, a redesign, more and better tests, etc. we struggle more to advance on the project.

The technical doubts on software face us sooner or later, precisely that is why we called them "doubts", because they are something that if it does not gets solved, they will take us more time and effort to solve them later or will cause unpleasant secondary effects.

And it is something we must see as something we got to take off as soon as possible. When I realize something like this, before starting with the next new functionality, I try to implement and solve everything that could generate some kind of technical doubt.

The day-by-day has many moments to obtain a little satisfaction: knowing that a problem has been solved or making a wonderful micro design are, for my at least, a little ray of happiness and satisfaction for the work done. We turn that well finished piece into a jewel that will later report us facility and commodity when it comes to solving problems.

» The planning of the project's phases is not stable

Sometimes I think if I just had bad luck, but this is just a personal reflecting: when I talk to people with a kind of dilated experience, I come to the conclusion that the same problems happen on many work environments.

It happens very often that, in the middle of the tasks of a planning, the project's manager decides at his "own risk" to change it. Perhaps there are good reasons for it, but if this happens very often it is a symptom that the team's manager, the responsible of planning the tasks, is not doing a good job. On software we organize with the tasks we have ahead in our minds: if those change continuously we will suffer an uncertainty that will negatively affect the work done. Since I am responsible of defining and planning those work phases, I carefully try to not get out of the established script, I don't always make it, but I clearly know that it is my responsibility to maintain the established planning during that time.

» Our work environment isn't calm enough to let us flow while we program

Not that we need a convent to work peacefully, but it is necessary that we have an environment that allows us to work with enough calmness and serenity. Not that long ago I read that on an open space (those open spaces in offices where we sit on large tables and can see almost everyone's faces) a worker received between fifty and a hundred "motives of distraction" during their workday. On Internet we can find a lot of different definitions but this is what I have personally experienced.

Sometimes when we program we are self-absorbed by our job, the same way as a writer who is developing a new chapter for his novel: this activity demands plenty of attention and concentration, how are we going to obtain them if we are always distracted? Someone may think "what a delicate people", well I am very sorry, but whether you are making a sculpture, writing a novel or painting a chocolate Mickey on a birthday cake, you will need at least one moment of concentration. Denying it is lying to ourselves. We cannot create with a disperse mind with which we cannot concentrate. I still do not believe that being able to think about two things at the same time.

» We do not domain correctly the technology used

Great ballast for working productively: if we do not know deep enough the technology we are using we cannot expect to make great progresses on the software we got to do. It is our responsibility to detect this gap and form ourselves or ask the company for formation to advance in our work. Is this is so, the team's responsible should delegate the critical tasks to the more experienced members and leave the least relevant for those who still don't manage the tools or technologies correctly, at least during that formation period. We see again how a management decision could ballast the productivity (and results) of a team.

But there is still something worse: converting the project of your first concept test with a new technology and, therefore, all the derived problems from inexperience will be present within it. I made that mistake many times, so now, every time I have to direct or start something with a framework, library or anything that I do not know well enough, I make the effort to make a complete prototype before overturning all that new knowledge on the final project.

» We do not have enough capacity to make the pending tasks with order

Working with order is fundamental. It is not weird to see those who jump from a task to another without completing them. Let's not talk about that we start with those that attract us most.

As programmers, jumping from a task to another, just as concentrating on a subject and then another, takes time. They say that when we lose concentration in something due to an interruption, we take at least fifteen minutes to return to the same level of concentration. If we flirt with several tasks at the same time we will need a lot more effort and time to complete them than if we just make them one after the other. On how to organize ourselves well, David Allen's books stand out in this regard.

I am sorry we are not parallel thinking beings; we can only

be very concentrated on a single subject at the time.

» We do not always have the adequate equipment, tools and environment

I have already started a chapter with that one traumatic experience in which compelling the entire project in which I had to work lasted more than five minutes on a PC "of the time". We have to demand what we need to work productively and with commodity. Sometimes it is our responsibility to detect these necessities because the team's responsible may not be aware of them.

» There is a time vampire in the team

We must root out those who simply do not let us work by causing continuous interruptions, are repeatedly asking for help, send stupid e-mails, etc. They are what I call "time vampires". Common sense tells us where is the barrier between the admissible and abuse. We have to be drastic on this: such a partner, no matter how much we like them, is sucking our blood, I mean, is not letting us be as professionals as we can be. We should try to be the ones who manage our own time and it should not be at mercy of the caprices and interests of others.

Productivity is often confused with working more and more hours. But trust me, increasingly, the number of hours do not matter, even if the current framework settles X weekly hours of job. Your prosperity, however, is not going to be based in the amount of time your work, but in the results you obtain from that time and how scalable it is.

Productivity is the capacity of working better dedicating fewer resources to obtain better results, the opposite of the chair warmer syndrome, the lack of organization, harsh working environments, continuous interruptions and the inexistency of a simple planning. The quality of what we produce is related with good productivity. It is like this in any job, even software development.

As we can see there are plenty of factors that determine if we work productively or not. Some of those are factors we have to control and manage; the others, on the other hand, are the team's and the organization's responsibility.

It is clear, then, that we do not produce more by working more hours, but bettering all the aspects productivity related that surround the work we do.

Nonetheless, this has a great economic repercussion. On 2016 I was punctually hired by a company with great growth as a quality consultor. The team was very good but lacked of experience in those matters; after a few contacts, I realized that the team and its management, suffered from each and every one of the illnesses pointed out in this chapter. The result was pissed off and stressed people, the impossibility of implantation of a real methodology and the incapacity to offer concrete dates for the great and new functionalities to implement, surely ballasting financial results.

We do not program in front of a computer screen and that's it: we need the adequate conditions to make a good job; sometimes what differences a company from another, between a project and other is not the technical quality of the team but the conditions that surrounds it.

Key points_

✓ When it is frequent and necessary to take extra hours to finish the job, we have a lack of team's productivity case in front of us.

✓ We cannot maintain the work's quality after a certain number of hours of extreme dedication.

✓ We are always looking forward making quality software and, for that, we have to solve productivity problems, some of which we mentioned in this chapter.

*About frameworks, libraries and how we reinvented the wheel_*

«There is no problem that cannot be broken down into smaller and more manageable ones». I remember this affirmation like if it was yesterday from Mathematical Algebra teacher from my first years at the university. This may look evident, but someone has to point it out to you for the first time so you can realize it and everything it involves.

In a way, this principle can be applied to our day-by-day on plenty of different scenarios. Sometimes we feel overwhelmed by a grey mental nebula in front of an unapproachable task and we know it can take us days or week to solve.

Notwithstanding, if we look carefully and with insight, we can see how this threatening nebula has parts; so as we look better those parts start to get better defined every time and if we look even further, we get to a point in which what was big and almost irresolvable before, is now a set of little problems that are easy to solve individually.

Suddenly we realize that what was huge and did not know how to solve before now has a solution and we can even anticipate to the moment in which everything is solved. What a relief...

This is just a simplified version of "divide and conquer".

Now well, the act of programming and solving problems through code is similar to this process, or at least it should be, and not understanding that is what gives place to those exaggeratedly big code files, classes with hundreds of thousands of lines (I have seen it) and monolithic projects that are extraordinarily rigid, fragile and coupled. A code is considered rigid when its design is very hard to change; also, a code is defined as fragile when it is easy to break down on many places as soon as the most minimal changes are produced.

Somehow, designing software consists on structuring a problem understandably and with well identified atomic parts.

The difference between a good programmer and a, let's say, novice developer is that when a big problem gets to the last one he immediately starts to write code lines. The first one anticipates better and, way before posing the name of a class or module, analyzes the problem they're facing and divides it on simpler and smaller parts; these turn into others even smaller, and it goes like that until all the pieces get the shape of a coherent mosaic that gives us enough confidence to start coding. Let's just say that this is a high level design act.   We still do not consider refactoring strategies and the application of good principles at this point: this conceptual decomposition of the problem is prior.

The interesting thing about this abstraction process is that it gets better the more experience you have; it makes you realize that many of those tiny parts have things in common and coincide, what results in its reuse.

Some time ago I was asked about the development of a simple web portal to be developed on ASP.NET MVC in which they had to integrate, among other thing, the insertion and obtainment of data bases images, authentication via Gmail and Facebook (...), validation of formularies asynchronously via Ajax and a long etcetera. Well then, some of those elements were fairly clear, and the others were completely unknown to me at that time.

Before getting started and begin with the application's general skeleton, I researched in detail sample projects with each and every one of those functionalities that I did not know how to face. Each one of those projects (some obtained on Codeplex and other on Github) was small, but solved a very specific problem that I could integrate later (after knowing all the internal details) on the general project.

Over time, this was growing orderly, with each of its functional elements well resolved, coherent and without loose ends, simply for having done the exercise of subdividing the general problem into parts. Along the way, I discovered many popular libraries that solved a large number of those particular problems.

This is nothing more than a simple example but we can apply it anytime we have something to solve with a minimum complexity.

I always say that software developers are some kind of translators: given a problem we convert it (translate it) into a design that will come with the code lines that solve it. The curious part of this process is that independently of the technology, languages or tools we use to solve a problem, the "mental approaching" to the matter are identical.

Our main fail, I insist, is avoiding this process of decomposition into smaller parts and want to approach everything at once because it is fun for some people to write code "anyway". We write code, ok, but we need a guide that indicates us that the process and the way of generating productive code is correct, the rest is pure improvisation with disastrous consequences on the quality of what we generate, the company for which we work or even our own professional career.

The more time we spend doing this planning job and seeing how to structure application in the best way, the faster we will advance later. I have seen it and experienced it over and over again.

It is of vital importance to our profession to know how to decompose the whole into smaller, individual, independent and totally decoupled part, and here is where we truly get to the crux of the matter: the habitual incapacity to develop software with a high decoupling degree. I do not get tired of repeating it because I think is something of vital importance, even more at a moment in which we have got over the monolithic conception of applications and think even more about of the independent services that implement it (third-party of implemented by ourselves).

We can even affirm that the quality of software is directly proportional to the level of decoupling achieved by each of its parts. I am surprised that concepts such as "coupling" and "rigidity" are not constantly coming into the mouth of software developers; maybe we like to play with emerging technologies better than mastering the fundamental tools for making code correctly (or, at least, in the best possible way according to the circumstances of each one).

Let's imagine for a moment that we are asked to develop a CRM for a client (customer relationship management) with some special particularities. What the client wants is a system that "works", that brings value and couldn't care less about what do we use and how do we use it to achieve it.

With a simple analysis we'll see that the product we are going to deliver has to have a user interface at the least, a sufficiently rich data model and a business logic that connects the user's interactions with managed and stored information.

Now well, "a user interface" is still a very wide concept, we lower the level and according to the client's specifications we will obtain the essential parts of the system, like clients management, supplier management, contacts management, and to connect them to the stock management of the company and a long etcetera. Going back on the same process, we will see that clients management implies being able to register new ones, modify the existent, distinguish between the types of client, etc. Shortly after we start doing this exercise, we would have decomposed an apparently big problem (the CRM development) into smaller parts.

How we manage, design and implement those "parts" will determine the success of our system, no more no less, I am afraid that this relationship is not always notice and I got to recognize that it is a little subtle.

The habitual temptation, especially among neophyte developers, is not getting to the parts' definition with enough granularities, so when it is time to codify, the coupling level between them is too big, if this decomposition job has not been already done by someone with more experience.

That is how stop leaving stones on the path shaped as code and modules "very similar" or duplicated, for example. If it continues like this, it will arrive at a system that may work, but when it undergoes the slightest modification on an island of its structure, another will jump through the air anywhere in the system in an unexpected way. Then we will have built something totally rigid for that client where absolutely everything will have been developed (except the database engine, let's hope). This is an end that, I'm afraid, happens a lot: the creation of an ad-hoc solution for a client where nothing, absolutely nothing is reusable and even worse, seen from the other side, nothing from other has been reused. I mean, this is an end, but who has not seen this approach with their own eyes in some way? Moreover, who has not fallen into that error some time?

If you work in a project where it is known that if something is touched in any part and nobody has the certainty that there will be no errors on other parts of the system, then you know there is a lot of work to do on the application's total redesign or even write it again from zero.

One of the skills we have to have to develop software is a great common sense, although sometimes we need a mentor (or a pile of books) to show us in what does this special sense consists that could help us perform our work better and with more efficacy.

We are effective as we "reuse" and write reusable code. This is one of my "mantra-quotes" that I repeat continuously.

Go back and read the previous quote: it has nothing to do with the way of implementing a module that solves something in your application, but about shaping it so it can be used as a library in other applications, its design, and the exposed interface will no look like anything else.

If we have achieved a set of parts sufficiently small and modular, decoupled between them and bringing certain functionality individually, we don't have to be very smart to find some patterns between those functionalities and maybe developments from previous projects. We have reached the concept of bookstore or library: we have finally reached the conclusion that there are common parts in many projects that, correctly isolated with no specific particularities, we can reuse over and over again, saving development time and supporting our solution on very proven and mature parts. So, we avoid to be constantly reinventing the wheel.

Another step on this "reusable functionality isolation" concept is proportionated by a work framework; in this case it is also established a set of practices to solve the set of functionalities with the same criteria and coherently. Most of the time we understand, because they are indispensable concepts of a software developer, what are libraries and frameworks and what are they for, without realizing that we have to work day-by-day with the same philosophy: isolating the functionalities of our applications as decoupled as possible.

Some months ago I participated on a project where the client (a hotel chain of the Balearic Islands) had a development team that had developed their own framework in the shape of common API to build above them all the applications they needed, with common methods to access the Oracle data bases, same log mechanism to all the applications and authenticated user with the same method, etc. A success of which I took good note.

Then we talk about working with productivity and

efficiency developing software we also refer to the need of looking for frameworks mature enough over which to build our projects. Moreover, it is not like that that computer science has evolved?, abstracting more every time, we find languages and tools every time higher that allow us to easily write applications. The goal is that the developer works principally centered in the project's requirements, not the infrastructure details or the low level, in the "plumbing".

Who has not ever written on a simple library to write log messages? Nonetheless, those are well known open use libraries like log4net (port de lo4j for .NET), Common.Logging and a long etcetera.

So it happens to the infrastructure of our project that we can support over well-known and consolidated libraries and frameworks.

Frameworks, libraries or modules are related concepts but they all imply the same: reusing, decoupling functionality from our projects and center on the requirements. Sometimes we reinvent the wheel due to the simple laziness of not researching what other have done successfully, or just because we want to do it ourselves.

We sometimes crash into that "programmer's laziness": Sometimes we find it more comfortable for us to do it ourselves than to look for someone who has thought of it before doing it in a general and elegant way, and who has also published it for general use under some type of open license.

If we fall into that kind of laziness believe me when I say that it will be very expensive in the medium term, then we will not only have to worry that the essence and what is important for the project works, we will also have to keep all those parts that we did not want to reuse and made by others surely better than by us.

I've been working with Node and Drupal for years (although the products we develop from the company are based on the Microsoft technologies), and what I like the most about those environments is the huge reusable module ecosystem created by the community.

In a project in which I've been working recently (started on 2017) using Node, I can count more than thirty different modules and libraries that with an infinite generosity, their authors have made available for anyone. Back in the day, it was indispensable that we had to develop all that functionality from zero. Moreover, some functionality that I have had to implement several times (and for which I have not found a ready-made solution that suits well), I've been isolating and publishing it as reusable modules in GitHub.

Key points_

✓ If we do not know how to face a specific functionality, it is better to do some research on a side project, not the general one. This way, experiments don't mess up the production code.

✓ We like to innovate, but on most occasions many utilities had already been created and made available by the community of developers with open licenses that allow us to use them.

✓ Our project will be more sustainable if we maximally decouple its functional parts.

✓ We should not try to reinvent the wheel, this only works to practice and experiment; on a serious project we have to know how to use to the maximum well-known, mature and consolidated libraries and frameworks.

*Good developers write debuggable code_*

Sometimes when people asks me what I exactly do, I found myself in trouble for not correctly synthetizing my current occupation, so I just end up answering that "I do software" or "I program". Well, actually, I am also involved on business development and the start-up of pilot projects.

The fact is that when I think about that answer I am actually telling myself that it is not completely true, because even if I spent all of my time developing software, programming, how much of that time is actually spent on writing "production code"? We understand as production code that code that actually solves the application's problems, which is executed when it is deployed to the client; nonetheless, it takes a lot of work to make a good quality production code, work in the shape of organization, discipline, good practices' application, formation, etc.

This is a matter confused by mane developers: we spent little time on actually writing new production code and dedicate the rest of it to the many other factors that "surround" this activity and we have described on The Black Book of the Programmer; notwithstanding, we don't give those other factors the relevance they have. I believe that thanks to those factors we can develop quality final production code.

What we like the most, maybe because it is the most creative part of our work, is sitting, solve problems programming, research this or that technology, etc., this is what I call the playful part of software development. Nonetheless, it would be naive and unproductive to try to spend all of our time on it.

So, what do we spend most of our time doing? At any activity, you need some kind of organization and planning if you really want to be centered. On software, unless you are developing a personal project you do to advance at times and just for fun (something I do continuously), the is normal that you are part of a development team; to work on it, you must dedicate time and effort to coordinate with your partners, attend meetings, revising the work of others and other similar tasks.

On the other hand, when we program we cannot obviate that if we consider ourselves professional developers, we have to support a big part of what we do with its correspondent tests; sometimes creating the adequate tests and execute them correctly can take us more than a half of our work time. Ok, there are people who have this role, the testers; although I am afraid there are actually few work teams with so differentiated roles. I think is obvious to repeat that we have to support with tests a big part of the code we write and, nonetheless, just a few teams make them naturally and without considering a cost.

Do we sit and start typing code like crazy? At all, any writing exercise has a work behind as well as planning effort and thinking minimally about an initial design to a greater or lesser extent. It is true that we have the impulse to get in front of our IDE as soon as possible, but we can only do this to make prototypes and not to "play at home".

There is another element and, by the way, it is nothing negligible: we spend too much time debugging and fixing errors. This is quite evident, but the implications of it aren't: why is it hard to detect errors sometimes? Why there are situations in which an error occurs in random production and is almost impossible to correct because there are no traces of how it happened? Who has not ever been through this? Moreover, how is it possible that errors occur when the application is already on production? And I am not talking about small bugs but actual crashes that bring down the system.

When you have some years professionally dedicated to software development, you have the opportunity of seeing a little bit of everything: amazing works and also solutions that end up in the trash before being completed. It is really hard to determine how to value the quality of good software: coverage metrics, elegant designs, etc. There are even some standards, but they are still something very subjective and many people hangs onto this subjectivity to defend their dubious quality work.

In my opinion there is an element that never fails.

The quality of a piece of code is directly proportional to the present debugging capacity. Simple as that and, in my humble experience, this does not usually fail. If the code is hardly testable then it is clear that it has to be improved.

We spend a lot of time correcting errors and detecting fails (nothing worse than those the aleatory appear as I pointed out before), looking for design defects, etc. Therefore, could there be any way of writing code that allows this detection activity and debugging of errors better than any other? Of course there is, exists and is a developer's obligation to write debuggable code, which can be easily corrected.

Like on many other occasions, what is common sense and evident, something everyone should agree on, is not so much when you have to apply it to your day-by-day. Writing code now that is easier to debug later, requires of a continuous effort for following the good practices of software development. Moreover, it requires of a different paradigm and a completely different way of thinking about programming. Not doing it this way will be something we will regret on time and effort when we have to start correcting errors (that will undoubtedly appear) or evolve the system. Let's say we enormously increase the technical doubt by not writing an easy-to-correct code.

In the development team that I am now leading, has happened to us that we have to go from writing a lot of unitary and integrative tests at the same time we write production code, when we have finished a work sprint and are about to close a version, the validation tests reveal many errors for which we have to spend plenty of time to solve.

Therefore, if the software we have to correct is hardly debuggable, the time to amend errors will be increasingly major. And time, actually, is our biggest professional asset. There is nothing more frustrating than spending a whole morning trying to figure out some bug that will end up being an authentic foolishness...

It is unavoidable to introduce bugs on the code, although we can minimize the time spent debugging.

A question I ask myself every time I think I've finished a task's implementation, requirement or user history is "everything I have done could be easily debugged by me or anyone else in a few months?"

There is a clear relation between a solution that can evolve (more functionality can be added to it) and a solution for which it is easy to correct or detect errors. Their intrinsic quality is determined for having followed or not some design principles and good software development practices, which are also well-known and documented since years ago.

In the software development literature, there are three books that, in my opinion, clearly serve to learn to write more clean and debuggable code, they are:

- ✓ "Clean Code" (by Robert C. Martin)
- ✓ "Code Complete" (by Steve McConnell)
- ✓ "Refactoring: Improving the Design of Existing Code" (by Martin Fowler).

We have already talked about them on The Black Book of the Programmer; every professional developer should have a copy of each one of these books at the head of their beds and, also, there should be an assignment about those topics in the computer enginery's certification or any other one where people is taught to "program".

S.O.L.I.D design principles, good messages and log traces, design patterns, anti-patterns detection, enough decoupling between the functional parts of the system or with similarities, functions or methods with relatively few parameters, correct election of variables' names, classes, etc., even a good structure and organization of the code on the solution. Everything, absolutely everything, facilitates the ability to solve and debug an application.

We defend the practice and everything clean code related precisely because it gives us the necessary skills, among other things, to generate an easily debuggable code.

To some extent, we can say that we learn to program debugging errors, but, do we have in mind the debugging capacity of our software while we develop it? Do we take any action in this regard? Do we really take it into account on a day-to-day basis?

There are several consequences from our application not being good enough to be debugged (all of them catastrophic); unsatisfied clients when the correction of something takes too long, more expensive projects because bugs are hard and demand too much time to be corrected, demotivated software developers due to having to spend an important amount of time to solve the errors (which also have a productivity cost) and a long etcetera. And it all generates an important waste of time, when we also are in an economic context where project's quotation proposals are based, almost exclusively, on the time dedicated to execute them and, therefore, an unsustainable application will subtract us competitive advantages.

Again we see how a software developer's productivity has nothing to do with the amount of worked hours, but with the capacity of writing sustainable and debuggable software.

We cannot be compliant and close a module or task without asking ourselves if we have done everything possible for the generated code to be debuggable enough. If it is, we stop accumulating technical doubt and we can dedicate more time incorporating new characteristics and useful code to the project. We will be, definitely, more productive and motivated.

Key points_

✓ Solving a problem developing software is not enough; the generated code has to be debuggable.

✓ The effort for writing clean code is a continuous job; we cannot lower our guard at any moment.

✓ There has to be an effort so the tests are well written and easy to maintain, too.

✓ As programmers we spend a lot of time fixing errors, it is something intrinsic of software, another reason to facilitate this job, which will make us spend more time writing production code.

✓ We are productive as we are capable of writing code that can be continued and corrected.

*Slave of your own solution or wanting to be indispensable_*

Throughout the working years of life one finds plenty of people, some turn into friends, acquaintances who come and go, you get to work close to some; definitively, you end up seeing a little bit of everything (or that's what I think even though I am open to the discovering of new surprises). There are people of the most normal and totally freaky people. Habile people, big professionals and humble, and others are the complete opposite (egotistical and proud).

As a software developer, you also find some kind of partners with a special pelage. We do not only build software but we also have a certain psychological idiosyncrasy, we like to be in power of what we do, making it ours and creating our special "power parcel". This behaviour, which may seem at first as nothing more than an understandable position to defend oneself, is more harmful than positive for the medium and long-term interests of a good developer.

So much so that, you may even find someone within a

work environment, who denies to "give you information" to make something work or keeps something inside a black box that only that person understands or can keep, keeping a captive business. This should be something punctual but it is a relatively common posture. At other times and for diverse circumstances, you are so good and efficient in something concrete that you get pigeonholed into a role that makes you a prisoner of it and impedes any other working or professional progress.

This is one of the biggest mistakes I have committed as a software developer. Some years ago I started to know a very specific product of an American company (Echelon); over time, I ended up becoming an expert on this product in which was also based the final solution in which we were working then. It was something extremely specific within the tele management sector of electronic counters (smart meters).

After one or two years, I knew it so well that I even helped the development team that worked from San Diego (California) to solve and detect errors. Up here all perfect, even though I was not aware that something fundamental was surging around me when enjoying all that knowledge about this product and to a certain extent the final solution depended on me. This "dependence" was not sustainable at all.

Naturally, I was quickly associated as the maximum expert on that product at my workplace who, also, knew how to use it effectively and with enough success for the project we were working on. I was always asked to solve any matter or problem related to the product. In the department, talking about it was talking about me: I was completely pigeonholed as an expert on that technology. What may seem good at the first sight is not so good in the medium term.

More than two years went by and I started to feel some kind of pressure personally because I noticed some technological trends passed me by because I barely had time to learn them; during that time, my dedication around this product and the final solution we developed based on it was total and I had no room to "other stuff"; logically I was not allowed to because my dedication to that project was crucial. My specialization in it was making me completely captive.

I started to wonder what did that mean at a professional level: was it good that I was so trusted on that area? Did it make me have more working safety within the enterprise? Were some other opportunities passing me by? Did I preferred safety or was I willing to pay some price to prove other stuff? Was that "security" real?

At the same time I was asking myself those questions, I intuited I was losing the train of some other projects and responsibilities: my bosses had me so pigeonholed into that specific area that giving it to other was too risky, or at least that was the impression I was getting.

On one hand, my success on the use of that technology

was making me captive of it; I was losing other working and professional opportunities within the same company, as simple as that; that's how I see it when a long time has passed since even though at that moment everything was translated into working dissatisfaction and an added stress. On the other hand, at times when I was seeing everything dark I had a fake safety sense thinking that the company could not do without me at any time. If I have learned anything on my life is that there is no one anywhere who is absolutely indispensable.

However, that situation I was living as a negative to my professional development tends to be perceived as desirable and even chased by some software developers. But it is a big mistake.

The, kind of twisted, reasoning is usually the following: since I am the only one who controls "this", because I know it better than anyone else or because I have done it myself and only I am capable of starting it, the company will never do without me and, also, my ego rises among my partners because I am the only one who "knows and controls" this and that, you feel like "they depend on you". Now I see it clearly that this is a behaviour pattern that some of my partners have repeated throughout hundreds of projects in which I have worked.

The same way, if you have successfully given birth to a solution, we have a hard time accepting that others come to assume it and evolve it, you feel like they are taking your prodigal child away from you, without realizing that it is not your solution, but the company's, that has paid you to develop it. You have to have a lot of professional maturity to assume it.

This is not good in my opinion and is also a complete mistake: a software developer cannot look under any circumstances for the "comfort zone" one feels when perfectly knowing a product or technology and from which one lives and that, sooner or later, will end up in the complete obsolescence.

A software developer must move at the same rhythm as technologic tendencies and, as far as possible, must participate on different projects throughout time, nothing worse than working on the same project for a long time. We are talking about that on software technologies five years ago was prehistory.

Leaving aside the technological dilettantism we exposed on the previous chapter, is it reasonable that a computer software developer nowadays ignores tendencies like data analysis, cloud services, big data, no SQL data bases, containerization of applications, micro services based architectures, etc.? Maybe yes, but then we are giving our selves some very short wings and our professional progression will drastically reduce.

When we want to make a living from a very concrete niche, like my case back in the day and that I have honestly set as an example, what we are actually doing is looking for a working safety parcel, but also reducing the anxiety that facing new things causes. This behavior is not well received in a sector in which everything, absolutely everything, is defined with a planned obsolescence beforehand, with very few exceptions.

A good software developer has written on his DNA the capacity of working on different projects, of pivot about technologies when required and the capacity of reinvent one's self to adapt to the new professional circumstances. Although it is said that the working world that awaits us is one of changing on several occasions the company we work to throughout our professional life, why don't we understand that we will change technologies, paradigms, methodologies and ways of doing and implant projects during all that time?

It could be objected that there are still who dedicate to maintain COBOL systems, and it is true, and I even know people who works with C to program control devices like remotes, but I would personally depress if I was told to spend the next ten years of my working life doing that exclusively, for example, although this is a very personal reflection.

Technology (and why not, society) advances with pioneers who take risks by proposing disruptive changes in a certain area, to a greater or lesser extent, there is where the opportunities are, not chasing a salary at the end of the month maintaining something we know enough but that makes us feel safe. Safety is not a fact, it doesn't exist itself, and it is a personal "sensation".

Opportunities come with movement and action: on our field this translates into working on different project and with diverse technologies as well as on different companies with different working scopes. I am not saying that we have to continuously change "yes or yes", but we have to identify when an exclusive dedication to something ends up ballasting our working opportunities and our professional progress, especially when we want to change and prove another kind of things.

The best professionals that I have met have changed companies several times, which does not imply that those who spent more time on the same one are bad professional, but it does reveal one symptom: a good professional treats himself as an enterprise, looking for the best project for his development, in the A company, or the B or as freelance.

Treating and managing our professional career like it was a company, is a concept that quite shook me when I first read about it on the book "Personal MBA" (by Josh Kaufman), a book that I highly recommend.

It could also be objected that on crisis times one clings to a burning nail, and so it is, logically (the developers just like anyone else, also have to pay the bills), even though mobility does not highlight anymore between companies but between the departments of the same company, at least on the environments in which I have moved until now.

The working paradigms are changing; if you have not

noticed... companies already know that it is more efficient to hire the just and minimal indispensable structural personal and punctually sub-hire freelancers, what means we will work on more projects and results. That's the way things are and in this scheme it has no sense at all wanting to cling to something concrete just to not stop being essential. Nowadays, and this is truer on software, nobody is indispensable: it is just a matter that someone who is at least just as woke as you and with some time ahead reaches the same knowledge and expertise level on a concrete product or technology, when not the company decides to literally throw it away and substitute it with something alike, which will surely be less expensive in the medium term that maintaining that product and you in the long term.

So, the code we write will be assumed by a partner that we surely won't know, for which it will be necessary to fulfill the sustainability parameters; this does not only consists, like I insist on The Black Book of the Programmer, on a software that has the capacity to be easily evolved, but also is that any person who knows nothing about it without too much effort could be capable of evolve it and maintain it; for that, it must be easily understood how the things on the project are made and structured: good documentation, design coherence, clean code, clearly seeing the design sense (like Robert C. Martin would say) and a long etcetera.

Key points_

✓   It is a mistake to make ourselves indispensables on a critical application for the company: it makes us captives of it and impedes our progress.

✓   Only periodically changing projects we will find better opportunities.

✓   Making the same tasks for a long time is unnatural for a software developer with concerns about progress.

✓   Feeling "safety" must be based on our technical effectiveness, self-confidence and a high self-esteem to know how to adapt to new projects and challenges, not on exclusively dominating a certain matter that is important for the company.

✓   We start a project knowing a priori that we will get out of it at some point; therefore, we will make sure other can easily assume it.

Learning from others (or how not to be a lazy developer) _

It is frequent that we are so self-absorbed by the software development we are generating that we have little time left to learn new technologies or "take a look" to other projects. It is relatively common that we spend too much time advancing on the same project.

We can read a good manual about some technology, from top to bottom and very consciously and, nonetheless, still have no idea of how to apply it to a real project; this knowledge is only given by experience and unlike other professions we fundamentally learn 2living and studying" the code generated by other, but, especially, directly working on projects. We can say we are C# experts but if we do not have the baggage of several projects with that language, our credibility will go down the drain...

One of the biggest vicious circles in which software developers incurred is dedicating almost exclusively and for a long time to the same project, where the architecture and way to do things, good or not so good, are more than established. We evolve the project with new characteristics, but always "within it".

I have lived this situation many times and one of the negative consequences is that you end up adopting an extremely rigid way to do things: when you start a new project, you tend to apply what you know better, which nothing more than the way you have spent more time is working on the previous project. That way you unconsciously repeat some architecture patterns (that you do not even think about improving), the same ways of organizing the solution, etc. It is not wrong, if you are a professional developer is because you do all that relatively well, but, are we sure we cannot do things even better?

Could a good novel author write without reading absolutely anything from other authors or books about narrative technique and attend courses and seminaries about the topic? Could a painter create a unique style without having drunk from the sources of other artistic schools? Could an architect improve a design without basing on what others have created? Therefore, could software developers improve our work without studying and seeing how other developers (surely more expert and smart) have solve a certain type of problems?

Although our profession insists on design maintenance, which is very important, it is often obvious that the reality we learn from fundamentally reading examples and code made by others. Simple as that and, notwithstanding, how many people have I not met who only and exclusively know the projects in which they have worked and, out of them, would not know where to start a new one; or well, solve all the problems they find searching on forums or abusing of Stack Overflow. This is a very common developer's profile, let's call it the "lazy developer", that one that out of one particular project or kind of projects would not know where to start.

The first problem of this "shortening of views" is that you tend to drag vices and bad proceeding forms to solve some situations, for example, you may be used to use an unique library for log messages' creation and ignore that there are plenty of those way more consolidated and better. It could be that tasks as simple like reading a simple archive you usually do it the way you are used to, until one day and almost by chance, you find out that there is a simple, efficient and elegant way to do the same with half the code lines. Or well you are used to it, because it was done like that at a certain time, to develop integration capes based on web services and now you find out that for some cases it is more convenient (and easy) to implement REST services. How were you going to find it out without looking at the code made by other on forums, projects or articles?

I got to recognize that sometimes I have noticed the same sensation writers describe as the "blank page fear" when I have had to start a project from zero. How do we organize the solution? Where do we start first? What architecture should we pose for started? Do we even how is it going to evolve in the future? Is a critical moment because the success or failure of the project will depend on the answers we give to those questions.

But, how can we learn this kind of things? We learn when we develop projects, that is obvious, what is not so is that we learn and tune our skills to "solve projects" by reading and analyzing what other developers have done; but for that we have to have a certain degree of humility.

The same way a writer discovers stylistic resources by reading other authors' books, a software developer finds new practical ways of doing the unimaginable, sometimes with great surprise.

For example, I had never thought using the chained calls styles they do on jQuery (a technical denominated method chaining); when I found this library, besides being amazed by its simplicity and elegancy, I found out that for some cases the chained calls style was a good technique, which has helped me to apply it more than once.

Each one has their own imprint or way of writing code; it is curious but, without going any further, the product in which I had worked on the last few years (Tele management platform and MDM IRIS), up to eight people have participated, and I can exactly guess who has done what without looking at the change control record...

A good software developer does not live exclusively

centered on the projects they're working on, but as part of their continuous formation process, they must read and analyze projects made by others. That way they learn styles, tricks and details that would hardly discover by themselves.

For that we must focus our work with some humility and be open to someone who can point you out how to improve this or that. The best developers I have met have been the humblest with their own work, the most open to knowing that there are better solutions one has not proposed. I always say that I hope someone pointed me out me errors daily: that way I would learn faster and better. I appreciate everyone who teaches me to do things better.

We live in a highly cooperative and open environment, with big shared resources and, nonetheless, many times we set out to solve projects "with the first idea that came to our minds". That is the first mistake of the lazy developer.

There is nothing better on your own curriculum than including a detailed list of projects and works in which you have participated: that heterogeneity will give a clear idea of your experience and versatility degree.

Key points_

✓ It is important (I would even say indispensable) to read every once in a while projects made by others. It could help us find better ways to solve problems.

✓ We should participate on a wide number of projects

during our working experience; we learn and improve as professionals participating on heterogeneous projects.

✓ Sometimes, learning about other technologies help us find other ways and techniques to do things that we can incorporate to the language or framework we use the most.

*Enhancing your productivity_*

When we talk about developing software, we do not refer only to sitting in front of a computer screen and write code lines. Throughout The Black Book of the Programmer we have seen infinity of elements that interfere, affect or allow the act of programming to be an authentic disaster or generate the conditions to produce quality software at the same time a developer spends time productively. If this is not clear yet, I suggest you read again from chapter one. The matter is that that software idiosyncrasy is not usually understood by the decision layers; the worst part is that sometimes not even the developers get it!

If you think programming is just writing code and do not understand how things like configuration management and integration help you improve the project's quality and to work productively, please keep on reading.

In a time when it looks like we praise the act of working more and more, I always say that it is not about spending many hours working but about being productive during the time we work, which has nothing to do. We have also clearly seen that the fact of dedicating many more hours chronically, day by day by day, on our working context, whatever it is, surely implies organization fails and that work is being done unproductively: productivity does not depend on working more but working better.

In the words on the amazing Raimon Samsó (you can find his books "The money Code" and "The Emerging Expert Class"), we are moving towards a new working paradigm in which success will be associated to talent, technology, innovation and, especially, the capacity of reinventing one's self continuously. On our profession it is easier to show those skills than others. The main thing is that we need to change our chips and not thinking about "fill with work" the eight hours or so of the working day, but we have to think about fulfilling an objective and get some results: we are not going to get paid for hours but for results; for that we have to work productively.

If you are like me and always have a personal project in hands (that ends up growing or not or generating a new source of income), spending your time efficiently is very important.

The indispensable tools and procedures of a good development team that is considered to be highly productive are a good configuration management and continuous integration; therefore, of the good implantation that we make of both concepts will depend to a certain extent to get more or less success in the project using the same effort.

Software's configuration management consists on the definition of a set of processes that support quality production at every step of the project, which implies a correct use of the version's control tool, how bugs are going to be managed, etc.

Do you think about the definition of configuration management at the beginning of the project? Almost never, I'm afraid and, therefore, it will come the time when you will have to pose questions that had to have been solved from the beginning, for example, how do we freeze this version before putting it in production for the client to keep on advancing in a minor revision? This kind of things are usually solved "on the progress", ballasting the project's quality and the productivity of work itself.

When there is a defined configuration management, that "way of working" we had on previous projects is usually dragged without realizing that every project, according to its nature, number of team members, estimated production deployment number, etc. requires of its own and specific configuration management.

And this is also where economic profitability of projects is when concepts like time to market (TTM) are more present every time, (it is time we spend putting in the market a new application's characteristic). It is about reducing this time to the maximum to have more business opportunities.

If those concepts are not correctly defined, we will lose a

lot of time throughout the project and the quality of what we generate will be resented, simple and overwhelming as that. We are more productive if at the beginning of a new project we set a moment to define, precisely, how the configuration management is going to be.

In the team I currently direct, we have established a simple norm that indicates how to "uplift" (check-in with Visual Studio or push if we use GIT) any advance on our development tasks: first, we actualize the project from the source code's version, then we compel, and if there are neither problems nor conflicts, then we "lift it up". Those easy steps considerably reduce the amount of code conflicts when there are a lot of people working on the same project. This is configuration management, the basic norms to work, but always thinking about reducing the potential problems to center on what brings value to the project.

In the best of cases, one of the team members is the one who does a timely following to work correctly according to the defined configuration management.

It usually happens when a new project is started, that we are excited to start to see something working, we see the planning of a correct and specific configuration management as a useless expense. Even worst when most of the projects start already delayed and rushing..., then it will be even harder to set a time to establish the functioning norms. Rushes always cause that things, paradoxically, take longer to complete with a worst quality at the end.

We should not start a new project without clearly establishing what are going to be the works procedures for it. It is a fundamental rule we must follow and it is surprising the little time and effort it takes to sit for a few hours and write the strategy to follow.

The biggest disaster I have known in this aspect was a department that developed software for embedded devices, with hundreds of clients around the world for which they had to procure a version of the project, with what changes, etc. it was a hell of a task; sometimes you could not find out what sources corresponded to what binaries for a particular project; no need to say that those who worked there lived completely stressed. It would have been solved since the beginning of the project if a correct configuration management had been established. How many unproductive hours were spent trying to solve this kind of problems? How many unsatisfied client? How much wasted effort (money)? There is always a well-organized work behind productivity and know-how; it is thanks to productivity we generate more income with less effort.

How many hours do we waste solving code conflicts because some team members has updated some changes done a week ago? for example. How much time has the project remained "broken" at the compilation level impeding the advance of it? How could have we soon detected that some parts of the project fail when you set them together, when they integrate to one another? How can we know as soon as possible that the project has stopped working or that some test has stopped successfully executing?

All of this, which was formerly done more or less manually (if it was ever done), is what the concept of continuous integration covers. The continuous integration's essence is reducing to the minimum this kind of problems, not losing time on conflicts that can be solved be themselves with a good working procedure, making sure that the compilation is always correct, which is fundamental for the team for parallel advancing and, especially, to detect as soon as possible when some tests have stopped working, because the more its solution delays, the longer it will take. Productivity, productivity and productivity that is continuous integration.

Just as in configuration management, the foundations for continuous integration are settled since the beginning of the project; of its good application and start up will depend that we lose from tens to hundreds of hours solving projects that would otherwise been avoided. Not in vain it is said that the best problem is that one that does not ever starts or that solves itself.

Continuous integration also assures a better code quality, because detecting the failed tests, allows us to solve them as soon as possible and makes us write correct code from the beginning.

If we are working on a personal project where we are the only ones developing it, it does not make any sense to start a detailed configuration management nor a continuous integration mechanism. For a team of two or more people it is indispensable to put into practice those mechanisms and, honestly, I do not see any other way to work coordinately without those tools on bigger teams.

I am afraid that sometimes the projects management only perceives the advance of it according to the number of written code lines or completed development tasks, without seeing that the definition and correct implantation of management configuration and continuous integration will increasingly accelerate the work and allow the developers to spend more time programming.

Luckily, it all gets better as the DevOps popularises more and more very time on the organizations' work culture.

Starting to work with defined configuration management procedures and develop our code tasks consistently with continuous integration could be something very shocking for someone who has always worked "their way", with the procedures "in mind" and without a clear culture of test's creation that prove that everything we have done works at all times. Once we take the step and incorporate those concepts to our software development culture, we get to a point of no return in which we do not think about going back at all, improving as professionals. Like they say, once you try, you never go back.

Key points_

✓ Working more hours does not make us productive, but doing the same job and with the same or even better quality in less time. The presentism at job is a problem, but as professional developers we only should look for working efficiently and search better results.

✓ Software developers are even more professional when they feel comfortable and know how to work under the umbrella of correct configuration management and continuous integration.

✓ If we land on a new working team in which this culture isn't assumed yet, we should indicate it, for everyone's sake...

✓ Continuous integration moves us away from the nefarious 20/80 proportion (80% of the time solving errors and 20% writing new code).

*The entrepreneurship era_*

Since long time ago I am trying to blend my working responsibilities with the start-up of diverse projects. Some technological and others, let's say, more traditional. Over time, some stay in simple frustrated attempts and other success, but what is undeniable is the enormous personal and professional richness that actively participating on those projects brings: in the end, they end up bringing value to any activity on your day-by-day.

Extracting possibilities from here and there to get to something useful turns into a habit, into a capacity "knowing-how-to-see" what others ignore due to lack of courage, fear to failure or, simply, comfort while waiting for a safe job that pays bills until the retirement pension comes. Nothing to object, of course, everyone has their concerns and choses their own options.

Not that long ago I read a reputed economist who said that we are passing from the commodity economy to the entrepreneurship economy: now we have to defend our own personal brand to achieve a temporal project or create a good professional reputation online.

The working paradigms are changing; we have repeated it many times throughout The Black Book of the Programmer; we have reached a new way of working, of bringing value, of creating synergies among teams, of new professions that did not exist ten years ago, of economic budgets by results and not by time, old and traditional sectors disappear or are reinvented with a completely new skin.

It is a great moment for entrepreneurship, especially for software developers.

On a recent report of a big service company about some working perspectives for 2014, they identify up to thirty new kinds of jobs that did not exist ten years ago and will be demanded from now to 2030. So, kinds of jobs evolve a lot, if you do not keep up to those demands you'll end up out of the market.

A great part of this brutal change is caused by the information technologies where the software developers have a leading role.

There are who perceive this change, this going out of our comfort zones as a terrible threat and live restlessly and constantly alarmed, but there also are who see it as a wonderful opportunity in which talent, creativity and professionality are essential. I always say that we went from presentism to talentism, from the rigid and receiving things flexibly to having to face them one's self. If you are hoping to find that job where you are told exactly what to do at all times, then you should know that it will be a shortage of it in the future.

I do not consider myself authorized to evaluate if this is good or bad; I think it will depend on the special idiosyncrasy and context of each, but what I am sure about is that there were never more opportunities to be successful:

✓ The entry barriers of many businesses have reduced or even completely disappeared.

✓ Many traditional activities only allowed to some elitist circles have been democratized; for example, do you need a publishing house nowadays to publish a book? No way, there are options at everyone's reach to introduce your work to the world and, also, you can directly hire a professional editor or translator so they help you with your project.

✓ From the mythical dusty garage of the first geeks we have passed to being able to publish a content blog almost "at the stroke of click" or starting a totally innovative idea at a derisory cost, or we can even order someone, on the other side of the world, the creation of a prototype.

✓ Classic financing sources also evolve: from the obsolete visit to the bank we get to the possibility of contact business angels ourselves, participating on crowdsourcing campaigns or looking for entrepreneurs and partners with similar concerns, all through the web.

If the idea is good, there never were more possibilities of getting started on the tools to materialize it.

The software developers have the luck of seeing this frenetic movement "from the inside" because many of the projects that are currently innovating have a strong technologic component, maybe because its natural environment is the wed, because as a foundation it needs at least a portal that gives it coverture or because whatever the nature of project is it is indispensable to make without the direct or indirect use of software applications more or less specialized.

Nevertheless, do we also take advantage of this new economy from the opportunities based on new technologies?

You need to have a great company's infrastructure to start-up projects that can function and even change the rules. Within a few years surely almost nobody will talk about WhatsApp and, nonetheless, it is used by millions of people today. Bloggers make an extra income writing and commenting about what they like, and the same is happening with Instagram. Neo-rural people move from a big city to a small town to live according their concerns, living on a web where they share and write about alimentation, healthy lifestyle and alternative therapies (The Alternative Blog). A rural shelter has always the complete sign on its door because with little effort they assure clients from their own web with a minimal inversion on marketing and SEO. We order transferences from our mobile telephone and even start to assume that the digital coins will change the financial outlook just around the corner. Others are centered on "connecting" people with plenty of applications. The cloud world allows us to work differently at more scalable environments, every time cheaper, safer and with more and more services we won't have to implement again. And is already been talked about a technologic revolution and even a paradigm change that supposes the use of blockchain.

The book by Chris Guillebeau called "100€ start-up" is filled with examples like this: I always say that it is not about launching a rocket to the moon, but about having our feet in the ground, thinking and trying to start up an idea with discipline, effort and perseverance.

This book is one of those personal projects that I started writing back in 2012, published in 2014 and now, at the beginning of 2017, I am turning into a second edition while I write these words. Essentially, the conductive thread of all the previous chapters is about learning how to work better on our profession to always center in what really brings a final value, not wasting our time and effort on unproductive filling tasks. There is nothing worse than getting paid for unproductive time or for a work that is thrown away.

This is an example that also the possibilities of the "knowledge society" and the "new information technologies": its direct publishing (through CreateSpace and Kindle Direct Publishing), without going through the filter of a traditional publishing house that selects you from a pile of other books, it is an example of how many activities are changing their skin.

Do we realize that software developers do not "suffer" this new economy because our job is a consubstantial part of it? Let's take advantage of this circumstance to bring progress to our society shaped as new ideas and projects to make it more human and better; in the end, this is what our job always pretends: bringing something useful to our final costumers.

There are many books about entrepreneurship, even though you can read more about it on my web:

http://www.rafablanes.com/blog/emprendiendo-proyectos-de-software

*Conclusions_*

This book started with the idea of answering the following question: what distinguishes a professional software developer from another whose career is filled with stumbles, frustrations and bad quality works? Since its first edition I have found again the dynamics I describe on The Black Book of the Programmer in the clients for whom I have worked as responsible of a software development team and business development for my own company.

Answering that question has been my humble pretension parting from the experience I've accumulated working directly on many projects (so many that I would struggle trying to number them) and also starting diverse entrepreneur initiatives. Curiously, many of the keys are equally applicable to other fields that have nothing to do with software as a technical activity: motivation, service, good organization, correct use of the tools we have at out disposition, collaboration and, especially, a lot of passion and vocation for what you do.

Writing a good software project, with quality, that fulfills the objectives (which implies a constant revision of the requirements, specifications or user's histories) resembles a marathon more than a short-speed race: while the first one is long and we get to the finish line at a rate and effort more or less constant, the second one is faster, yes, but improvised and frenetic to reach the finish line at all costs.

From a non-technical but human point of view, the best software developers I have met (and those I don't personally know but I have through their books and articles or GitHub projects) are clearly distinguished by showing an extraordinary passion for what they do, by the "love" they put into an elegant, fine, functional and useful solution for the final users. They can pay us for doing any job as developers; nonetheless, it is undeniable that if we do not feel passion or don't believe in the project we embarked ourselves into, we are hardly going to achieve a better result: the project will be done, but "mercenarily" and with a lot of technical debts (that in the end always translate to extra costs, a burned-out team and a kind od expensive project).

It is undeniable that a bad management style will hugely influence the development team that is in charge of executing a project: I always say that a manager's first priority is to "facilitate" the job realized by the team members, as we analyzed on The Black Book of the Programmer. We are sailing in the same ship, so we should look for good managers (bosses) who know how to make their job correctly: we should run away from the "whip – boss" who thinks that writing code lines requires the same abilities as fabricating screws; precisely, "the screw factory" is a metaphor I often use to refer to those companies (big and small) the focus software the same way as in metallurgy: they can produce technological products, yes, but with the same methods... it is required a completely different work culture.

When we finish our academic formation we feel calm and relieved of having finally got over those exams, assignments we did not like and the face of some professor who we will hardly be seeing again. And yet, the true background career starts in the exact moment: all that learning time leads to a continuous formation in which we will be changing paradigms. We have seen how some social and organizational skills powerfully affect the result of our creative work.

Things being that way, I observe how most of the programmers exclusively cling to what the work that pays their salary every month requires: can we turn into professional software developers without knowing those technologies, without reading one book a month, nor assisting no seminaries, without learning from those who expose their works altruistically on the Internet? Of course not. Not at all.

What team are you into? In the one that advances with pushes with what they demand from eight to five or with that of the restless minds that point out articles in blog entries to read them in their free time on weekends? If you are a part of the first group, I am sorry to tell you that you will be out of the market sooner than later and you will have to dramatically reinvent yourself sometime.

Work paradigms change: sometimes we do not realize that we ourselves can cause the same disruptive technology that generates a new paradigm. Node.js and its author Ryan Dahl come to my mind; people like Ryan, with their brilliant ideas and projects, are who make our sector advance and information technologies are also changing the economy globally. Without going any further, thanks to Node I have started two entrepreneur projects (Green Kiwi Games and Picly.io) and a new start-up.

And what about Satoshi Nakamoto, whoever he was? One of the drivers of bitcoin whose blockchain technology is behind what some say will be the next internet era.

We live in the entrepreneurship era: globalization (or "super-globalization" that Trías de Bes would mention in the book "The Big Change") takes the manufactured working hours to Asia, for example, so the "developed" countries or innovate, undertake and we put the batteries on or our work will be equally exported. It is a matter of costs, simple arithmetic that puts at anyone's reach the externalization of almost any service (thanks, paradoxically, to the same technology we are dedicated to).

In any case, I think the glass is more full than empty: the

opportunities, businesses, new professions, new ways to do things, new services are there to the reach of who starts "thinking by one's self" and, the best part is, that all this economic paradigm change is supported by software itself, directly or indirectly.

A programmer more opportunities as anyone else of innovating and undertaking is this technological world precisely because of the knowledge of the tools and bricks that are being used to create this new global economic architecture. What do we do in the meantime? We can get beneficiated by this new wave executing the projects from "others" in the best of cases or well, we can get on it directly. The society's information atoms are hundreds of millions of code lines written by software developers who, like us, make everything else function.

The Black Book of the Programmer has showed you the abilities a good professional developer must have (curiously, many of them are not technical) and at the same time, the errors we have all committed at some moment and that have ballasted the quality of the projects or our own working and professional evolution. I hope that after reading it you'll be an even better programmer and know how to focus and direct better your next steps as a highly productive software developer.

Improving in our profession, in the project in which we are working on, in everything, is practically a matter of habits and, as such, they can be learned. Throughout the chapters of this book I have pointed out the more relevant and that any developer should incorporate to write quality software and, therefore, have a successful career.

*One last thing_*

As you probably noticed, this is not a book exclusively for programmers, it is also for those who have the responsibility of managing teams or work closer to the business development of a company in which software intervenes one way or another. The same way, if you have spent too much time in the profession, you probably have read about topics that, without a doubt, are part of your day-by-day, although it is convenient from time to time to stop and reflect on them and never forget the why of things.

Writing a book sometimes implies the deployment of too much energy and using part of your time to create something that you think will be useful for others. The same happens with this second revision.

If you actually found this work useful and you liked it, I would appreciate a positive comment on Amazon, because of that thing about social karma...

http://mybook.to/elndp

Thank you; and I hope that you will like my next publication more. See you soon at www.rafablanes.com

Seville (Spain), february 1st, 2017

The highly productive software developer's test_

The spirit of The Black Book of the Programmer is indicating what usually impedes producing quality software, influencing on the aspects that are not necessarily technical but especially relevant for the project's progress, be this personal or within a company's context. A good project is so because it has been made productively, knowing how to take advantage of good practices, most of them easy to develop, and incorporating the good habits of a good developer every day.

Up next we collect shaped as question the essential parts discussed and profoundly analyzed on the previous chapters. With the answers to the next questions a software developer and a team will detect all the possibly improvable areas of its daily activity or well they'll find gaps to cover and solve.

Some tests may seem obvious for more advanced working teams; others not so much, even I consider them equally important. The set, in the end, is what matters.

1. Is the code generated by us supported enough by tests?
2. Does the team we work with have enough test creation culture?
3. Do we consciously take some time to refactor? this is, do we frequently pose questions about whether something can be improved or simplified?
4. Do we leave comments like "to do:..." all over the code that won't ever be completed?
5. Do we look for applying S.O.L.I.D, KISS, etc. principles daily?
6. Does the development team work with enough calmness inside a cordial and creative environment?
7. Is there enough cordiality between the team members to cooperate on the project?
8. Do the projects we work on have to be finalized by "the day before yesterday"? I mean, do we always work in the rush?
9. Do we always look forward to work with the people who know how to cooperate and teamwork?
10. Are there individualisms in the team or people who find it difficult to work in a team?
11. Do the managers encourage a good climate in the working team and put all the means so it advances correctly?
12. Do we intentionally apply design principles when we program?
13. Do we tend to simplify something that already works?

14. Do we feel the need to fill with internal comments the code pieces we write?

15. When somebody retakes our job, do they have to be continuously asking for details they do not finish understanding?

16. Do we look for the mastery in those technologies we think we know enough?

17. Do we consciously apply the tactics described on the book by Martin Fowler about refactoring?

18. Do we correctly evaluate libraries and extern components that are used on our project and are aware of its evolution degree, maturity, user's community, etc.?

19. Do we adequately isolate libraries and extern components in our application for not having to depend excessively on them?

20. Are we aware enough that the project we work on will be required to change and those should be on proportion to its success?

21. Do we have a tendency of using always the last "yes or yes" without considering if its use is appropriate (and safe) in our project?

22. Do we prefer to use mature technologies instead of incipient and highly evolvable technologies?

23. Do we consider the risk of using relatively new modules, libraries and components on our projects?

24. Are we willing to profoundly modify a piece of code in

which we were working for a long time?

25. Do we try to maintain a code piece at all costs knowing it could be improved?

26. Are we honest with ourselves when we get to the conclusion that it is better to start something from zero than forcing the incorporation of the characteristics in whatever way?

27. Do we accept including more people into the team at times of crisis when the delivery dates are near and it seems like there is no way of completing the work?

28. Do we warn our responsible about the lack of resources to execute the project with quality and success?

29. If we are responsible of a team, do we have clear that when a team fails it is our responsibility?

30. Do we suffer of too many improvised meetings?

31. Do the meetings end up lasting much longer than the established time and are more topics discussed than those included in the agenda?

32. Do we always make a task that was planned by the project's manager beforehand?

33. Is the methodology or good practices overlooked in times of special stress or crisis because of the expected dates?

34. Does the manager change the project's criteria continuously?

35. Do we have all the necessary means to make a good job?

36. Do we start a new project or development phase by solving the most complicated or most disturbing parts?

37. Do we continuously apply refactoring to the work done or only when we remember it?

38. Do we always work with the same idea of quality in mind, which means, always wanting to do the best job?

39. Do we dominate the used technologies well enough?

40. Do we stick faithfully to the methodology used from the beginning to the end of the project?

41. Do we abandon good methodologic practices when we feel under pressure?

42. Do we work in teams with unbalanced talents, that is, some are very good and others very "bad"?

43. Are we working establishing a rigid general architecture at the beginning of the project when all requirements are not yet clear?

44. Is the general architecture of the project flexible enough to be able to modify it during its development or is it extraordinarily rigid?

45. The established methodology has been decided to be followed or ignored at the first moment of change solidly established?

46. Is the extracted profitability correctly following a methodology clearly perceived?

47. Are the most boring or routine tasks always relegated to the end?

48. Do we care enough that our software product is well done and works and also that it appears?

49. Do we put enough emphasis on the design of agile,

intuitive, friendly and elegant user interfaces?

50. Does it often happen to us that we design user interfaces thinking more about the developers themselves than the final users?

51. Do we know very superficially many technologies but very few in true depths?

52. Do we focus more on knowing something about many technologies than on solving real problems with our software?

53. Do we feel the need to use the last of the last on a new development just because?

54. Do we indicate in our curriculum the problem we have solve with our software or well a string of technologies we only know superficially?

55. Do we have all the work planned out with enough anticipation?

56. Is it common to arrive at the office without knowing exactly what we have to do?

57. Are the tasks that we have to take care of marked out?

58. Do we continually suffer interruptions during our work?

59. Do we have the resources and means necessary to carry out our work correctly?

60. Do you frequently perform extra hours to complete tasks?

61. Do we perceive that our manager cares enough for us to work concentrated most of the time in our tasks?

62. Do we try to reuse sufficiently mature frameworks and

libraries in the development of our projects?

63. Are we concerned that the functional parts of the application are sufficiently decoupled from each other?

64. Do we like to reinvent the wheel instead of using libraries that already do what we need because we believe we will do better?

65. Do we always strive to write code that is easy to debug and correct?

66. Are our solutions impossible to debug and correct when they are released to production?

67. Do we spend a lot of time working on the same project and using the same technologies as some years ago?

68. Do we periodically rotate from projects?

69. Do we detect in the team or department those who keep secret some knowledge and information about a solution?

70. Are we highly indispensable in a very specific and critical task that we carry out in the company?

71. Do we have an attitude of sharing with others everything we do or what we know best?

72. Do we review projects from other developers?

73. Do we often read development articles about the technologies we use regularly?

74. Do we participate in heterogeneous projects?

75. Do we start some type of configuration management before starting a new project?

76. Is the management of the defined configuration

faithfully followed throughout the entire development time of the project?

77. Do we practice continuous integration in working groups of more than two developers?

78. Are all team members aware of the importance of working faithfully with the continuous configuration and integration management procedures defined?

*Bibliography_*

I can consider many books as foundational to having written The Black book of the Programmer; you could see that many of them have nothing to do with software, but with different ways of "thinking" to front face your job, innovate, undertake and follow what you really want in your life.

Some of them are reference books for me that I read often and with each new reading I learn a new gem of wisdom to apply in my daily life. Surprisingly, in this activity in which seems to be is reinvented every year, the authors of some of these fundamental texts already have a few gray hairs.

ANDREW HUNT / DAVID THOMAS: "The Pragmatic Programmer"

CHAD FOWLER: "The Passionate Programmer: Creating a Remarkable Career in Software Development"

CHRIS GUILLEBEAU: "100€ startup"

DAVID ALLEN: "Organized Success"

ERIC FREEMAN & ELISABETH ROBSON: "Head First Design Patterns"

ERICH GAMMA: "Design patterns: elements of reusable object-oriented software"

ERIC RIES: "Lean Startup: How Relentless Change Creates Radically Successfull Businesses"

FERNANDO TRÍAS de BES: "El Libro Negro del Emprendedor"

FERNANDO TRÍAS de BES: "El Gran Cambio"

DANIEL H. PINK: "Free Agent Nation"

GENE KIM: "The Devops Handbook"

JOHANNA ROTHMAN / ESTHER DERBY: "Behind Closed Doors: Secrets of Great Management"

JON BENTLEY: "Programming Pearls"

JONATHAN RASMUSSON: "The Agile Samurai: How Agile Masters Deliver Great Software"

MARTIN FOWLER: "Refactoring: improving the Design of Existing Code"

MAX KANAT-ALEXANDER: "Code Simplicity"

RAIMON SAMSÓN: "The Source of Money"

ROBERT C. MARTIN: "Clean Code: A handbook of Agile Software Craftsmanship"

ROBERT C. MARTIN: "The Clean Coder: A Code of Conduct for Professional Programmers"

ROBERT C. MARTIN / MICAH MARTIN: "Agile Principles, Patterns and Practices in C#"

SERGIO FERNÁNDEZ: "Vivir sin Jefe"

SERGIO FERNÁNDEZ: "Vivir sin Miedos"

STEPHEN R. COVEY: "The 7 Habits of Highly Effective People"

STEVE KRUG: "Don't Make me Think: A Common Sense Approach to Web Usability"

STEVEN MCCONNELL: "Code Complete: A Practical Handbook of Software Construction"

TIMOTHY FERRISS: "The 4-hour Work Week"

Referencies_

(1) *Free Agent Nation*

By Daniel H. Pink

(2) *Continuous delivery*

http://en.wikipedia.org/wiki/Continuous_delivery

(3) Obsolescencia programada

http://es.wikipedia.org/wiki/Obsolescencia_programada

(4) *Building Microservices*

By Sam Newman

(5) *Software rot*

http://en.wikipedia.org/wiki/Software_rot

(6) *Code Simplicity*

By Max Kanat-Alexander

(7) *Stand-up meetings*: reuniones muy cortas para indicar «rápidamente» el estado de cosas.

http://en.wikipedia.org/wiki/Stand-up_meeting

(8) *The Passionate Programmer*

By Chad Fowler

(9) *Cowboy Coding*: forma de codificar sin estructura

metodológica alguna, útil para experimentación y pruebas. http://en.wikipedia.org/wiki/Cowboy_coding

(10) No Me Hagas Pensar (*Don't make me think*)

By Steve Krug

(11) Inversión de dependencias https://en.wikipedia.org/wiki/Dependency_inversion_princple

(12) Manifiesto ágil

http://agilemanifesto.org/principles.html

(13) *Done means done*: agile development principle by which a characteristic must be completely closed to continue with the next one, which implies having developed it with all its details, proven and accepted as finished.

www.ingramcontent.com/pod-product-compliance
Lightning Source LLC
Chambersburg PA
CBHW071108050326
40690CB00008B/1151